CONSCIOUS
LEADERSHIP

NEIL SELIGMAN

CONSCIOUS LEADERSHIP

REVEAL YOUR POTENTIAL.
INSPIRE EXCELLENCE.

WHITE LION
PUBLISHING

Brimming with creative inspiration, how-to projects and useful information to enrich your everyday life, Quarto Knows is a favourite destination for those pursuing their interests and passions. Visit our site and dig deeper with our books into your area of interest: Quarto Creates, Quarto Cooks, Quarto Homes, Quarto Lives, Quarto Drives, Quarto Explores, Quarto Gifts or Quarto Kids.

First published in 2019 by White Lion Publishing
an imprint of The Quarto Group
The Old Brewery, 6 Blundell Street
London N7 9BH
United Kingdom

www.QuartoKnows.com

A catalogue record for this book is available from the British Library.

ISBN 978 1 78131 932 1
Ebook ISBN 978 1 78131 933 8
10 9 8 7 6 5 4 3 2 1
2023 2022 2021 2020 2019

Designed and illustrated by Stuart Tolley of Transmission Design

Printed in China

For Jack,
and all those who stand for a kinder world.

CONTENTS

INTRODUCTION

Conscious Leadership is the journey out of fear.

It is a journey of self-discovery, adventure, inspiration and revelation, promising a growing appreciation of your brilliant self as you travel towards a clear and fearless state of mind.

All are welcome on this adventure, because you are a leader, whether you know it yet or not. You are a leader at work, in your community, at home and of yourself as the guardian of your choices, words and actions. You are a leader, whether it appears in your job title or not. You are a leader, even if nobody recognizes it yet but you and me. You are the creator of your impact, large or small, and each of your thoughts, words and deeds are at this very moment moving as ripples through the connective matrix of this world. Participating with awareness in this process is what makes you a leader. Nothing more, nothing less.

For millennia, human beings have been on similar journeys of self-discovery, pursuing knowledge, power, health, wealth, purpose, happiness and excellence. The human drive to look outwards, go further, run faster and build taller continues to inspire amazing feats of performance, science, engineering, medicine and technological mastery.

Yet while the human race has achieved great things, we have also fearfully led our world towards significant problems, environmentally, socially and politically. Our societies work well for some and poorly for many, and we find ourselves poised at a moment in history where fresh solutions can only emerge from an entirely new paradigm of leadership consciousness.

The world is crying out for leaders who are conscious: aware, awake, connected. We need leaders that understand that leadership is not about *I say and You do*, but about *I welcome and we create*. In short, Conscious Leadership is first on the dancefloor of presence.

This then is the new paradigm of leadership that you are invited to investigate, co-create and move into your world. While Conscious Leadership sets the bar high, it also meets you exactly where you are. There are no access requirements apart from a curiosity to explore and the courage to look within.

The first chapter of the book offers the foundations for Conscious Leadership

You are the creator of your impact, large or small, and each of your thoughts, words and deeds are at this very moment moving as ripples through the connective matrix of this world.

by outlining tools and practices to build Self-Knowledge. These include developing a vision for your future, identifying your values, considering the concept of right action and communicating your goals, needs and desires effectively. In the Self-Maintenance chapter, the focus shifts to the human body and mind as we consider how to optimize and fully explore the physical form through which we express our lives.

In the Self-Management and Self-Development chapters, you are invited to refresh your knowledge and build new skills to enable you to deal well with stress, change and the ups and downs of life. Outlook and mindset are also supported

here as the importance of happiness, emotional intelligence, self-compassion and gratitude are underlined. The final chapter, on Self-Realization, draws together all of the work that has been done over the course of the book and offers insights on excellence, alignment and leading others.

Your guide on this journey is no guru or master but a fellow traveller offering a set of time-tested principles, lessons and theories that may provide inspiration for your next step. At every stage you remain the captain of your own vessel, and it is you who selects your next move.

Whether you lead a business of thousands, are at the start of your entrepreneurial journey, or are a worker, teacher, parent or student, remember that ultimately leadership is how you engage with yourself, your choices and the people around you.

More subtly, it is the vibrational impact that arrives with you when you walk in the room, felt by others before you even speak.

Wherever you are on your leadership journey, this book aims to champion your efforts by providing theory, direction and companionship on your path.

HOW TO USE THIS BOOK

This book is organized into five parts and twenty key lessons, covering the most inspiring and valuable topics for Conscious Leaders today.

Although the process works most effectively if you start at the beginning, do feel free to jump ahead to a topic with which you feel most engaged, and explore from there. If a lesson does not resonate with you, do not worry. Move on. It may call you back if the time is right. For the path of Conscious Leadership is neither linear nor well-trodden. It is as unique as you are.

Each lesson introduces you to an important concept,

and explains how you can apply what you've learned to everyday life.

As you go through the book, TOOLKITS help you keep track of what you've learned so far.

At BUILD + BECOME we believe in building knowledge that helps you navigate your world. So, dip in, take it step-by-step or digest it all in one go – however you choose to read this book, enjoy and lead the way.

Specially curated FURTHER LEARNING notes give you a nudge in the right direction for those things that most captured your imagination.

CONSCIOU
LEADERSH
JOURNEY
FEAR.

S

P IS THE

OUT OF

SELF-KNOWLEDGE

LESSONS

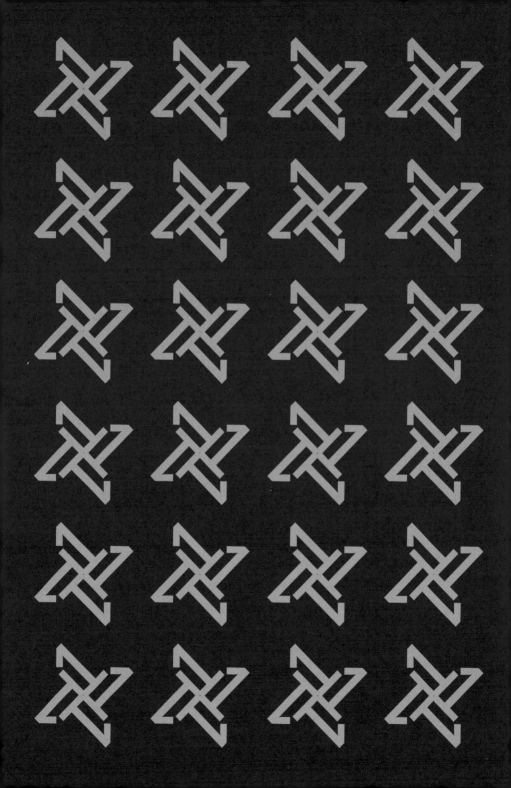

Your personal truths are revealed over time as your essential nature emerges through the context of your personality, circumstances, socialization and lived experience.

Coming face to face with the words 'self-knowledge' at the beginning of a book on leadership might feel a bit alarming. Yet self-knowledge lies at the heart of everything we do – and, crucially, why we do it.

Without a little self-knowledge, how could you even try to follow the words of advice so often attributed to Oscar Wilde?

Be yourself. Everyone else is already taken.

To be yourself assumes that you already know the length, breadth and depth of who you are. Yet self-knowledge cannot be downloaded from the Cloud on a quiet Sunday, nor is there a comprehensive user manual to let you in on your likes, preferences, strengths, weaknesses, desires, learning points and projected history.

Instead, your personal truths are revealed over time as your essential nature emerges through the context of your personality, circumstances, socialization and lived experience. The reactions of those around us, and the feedback we receive formally and informally from friends, colleagues and acquaintances, also help us to realize who we are. Self-knowledge then is something

that we learn quietly and gradually, by living our lives, and paying attention to our daily experiences.

Let's look at this from a different angle. Businesses and organizations must also consider carefully who they are, and why they do what they do. Brands make two promises to their customers: one functional and one emotional. To take one example, the functional promise of a high-end airline is to fly customers from A to B. Based on how they advertise, we might guess that their emotional promise is that the journeys taken by customers will be characterized by comfort, style, reliability, safety and quality.

Now imagine that you are a brand. What would your functional and emotional promises be? What tasks can the world rely on you to do? How do you think the people around you feel as you are interacting with them and delivering your functional promises? (Does this match up with how you hope they might feel?)

These types of reflections, although they may seem abstract, open the door to increased self-knowledge, which in turn forms the foundation of what you offer others as a leader.

VISION AND VALUES

Consciously moving through a nuanced and ever-changing world requires intention, direction and a practice of wise decision-making. It generally takes a little work and dedicated reflection to discover what the deeper drivers in your life are, and to name what you stand for. Investing time in doing this work now sets you up for success as you move forward on the journey of Conscious Leadership.

Your life's vision is a declaration of who you are becoming and describes the future that you are stepping into. Those that live with vision have an intentional direction to head in and are committed to increasing their self-awareness; they open courageously to their potential, look with hope to the future and forgo playing small. Creating your life's vision therefore requires a certain fearlessness and an open heart.

Your vision and personal values will evolve with you over time, so consider the following exercises as explorations, or research and development. Your answers today are not set in stone, so do not spend too long, just have a quick go. Gather the words, images and ideas that resonate most. You can fine tune them later as you are inspired to do so.

+ EXERCISE

Take a deep breath, settle into your seat and imagine for a moment that you are floating forward in time. It is now some years ahead and your life has moved on in a wholly surprising and delightful way. As you see yourself in this future you notice that you look rested and happy. Your mannerisms and movements have an easy quality. Your body feels fluid. The tightness in your shoulders has opened. Your forehead feels relaxed and your mind feels spacious too. Your thinking has become more potent, mature, insightful.

As you open to this future, you smile as you notice that you are happy, healthy, strong and vital. You feel energized, dynamic, bold and confident. More than this, you notice a new depth to your compassion and love. You feel light. You are offering your unique contribution joyfully to the world. It feels effortless. Exactly right.

Now, ask yourself the following questions in turn. You may wish to close your eyes to increase your focus, then jot down what you notice. All impressions and answers are valid.

01. In this future, where are you?
02. Who is with you, playing a part in this vision?
03. How do you spend your time?
04. What do you do?
05. What looks or feels different?
06. Is there anything else you wish to remember from the vision?

1. Costa rica
2. My day surrounded with friends.
3. Working in my creation.

NAME YOUR VALUES

Identifying and taking ownership of your values will offer you a compass with which to navigate the complexities of new business decisions or dealing with a pivotal moment in a relationship. Charting a conscious path through your life and as a leader requires careful decision-making as you weigh up impact, benefits, risk and costs. Your values describe what is most important to you and what you stand for. When tough decisions arise, or times of uncertainty or conflict, they can be consulted and will keep you centred in your integrity.

Businesses use vision statements to describe the future they hope to create. My own company, The Conscious Professional, holds a vision for *conscious businesses populated by enlightened executives*. While the vision may or may not come to fruition in my lifetime, it offers us a clear direction to move in and helps us make decisions that are in line with our intentions.

Holding a clear vision for your life can do the same for you. You already have some data from the Build exercise, and now it is time to consider your vision with a clear intent. Your vision statement might focus on you, your hopes and dreams for the future, your family, your friends, community, business, society or even the planet.

EXAMPLES
- I hold a vision for a life filled with fun and adventure.
- I hold a vision of leading an innovative company that changes the future of commodities.
- I hold a vision to be the best lawyer in the country.
- I hold a vision of becoming more confident and moving freely into the next chapter of my life.
- I hold a vision to be of service to my family and community.
- I hold a vision of working alongside the greatest minds in the world.

YOUR TURN
- Reflect on all of your answers so far and make a note of your vision statement.
- 'I hold a vision...'
- Now try saying it out loud.

Now you have your vision statement, it is time to reflect on the values that will guide you on the path ahead. Ask yourself – what is most important to you right now? Choose three words from the compass that best describe your current values, adding your own if you wish. Record them in your notes.

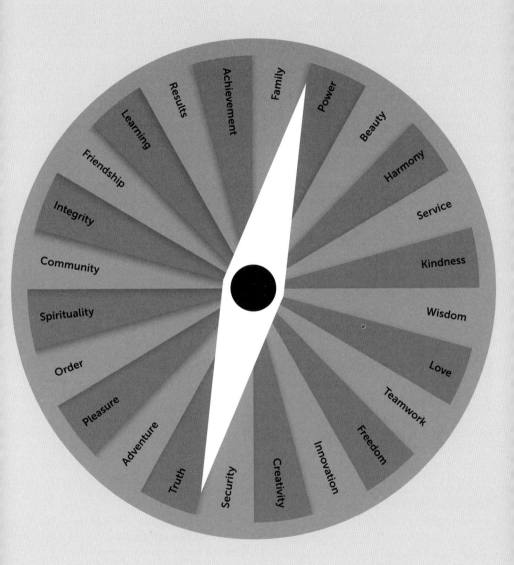

Family
Power
Beauty
Harmony
Service
Kindness
Wisdom
Love
Teamwork
Freedom
Innovation
Creativity
Security
Truth
Adventure
Pleasure
Order
Spirituality
Community
Integrity
Friendship
Learning
Results
Achievement

MISSION

A clear vision is just the start. The next challenge is to take your ambition and translate it into action. Not just one, but hundreds and thousands of small, consistent, courageous actions. You are probably doing this already, so consider the next exercise a tune-up.

Let's start by considering the concept of Right Action.

Right Action can be defined as 'actions in harmony with the whole' and can be used as a practical aid to decision-making in addition to your values.

As a leader and as a human being, you will find yourself frequently at the proverbial fork in the road. At this critical moment, Right Action asks you to consider three things: the individual (I), the group (us) and the whole (all of us).

In practical terms, if you are making a decision you need to consider:

01. **Yourself (Egocentric)**
02. **Those immediately impacted (Ethnocentric)**
03. **The wider community (Worldcentric)**

For any dilemma, challenge or problem, this process invites you to seek out a solution that takes account of the ripple effect.

Many people in the corporate world will be operating in firms that do not yet recognize the value of this approach, instead being more aligned with the egocentric approach. If that is you, and you are thinking that this sounds impossible to change, that is why it is called leadership. Leadership often requires you to point in a different direction, to move against the grain and to forge the new in the crucible of criticism and struggle. Perhaps this was most eloquently put by Gandhi when he said: 'Be the change you want to see in the world'.

RIGHT ACTION IS

- **Doing what you love, in the most exciting place, in a way that helps others.**
- **Sitting quietly until harmonic clarity arises.**
- **Brainstorming with those impacted before you make the decision.**
- **Saying no, when everyone else in the room says yes or says nothing.**
- **Being the change you want to see in the conversation.**

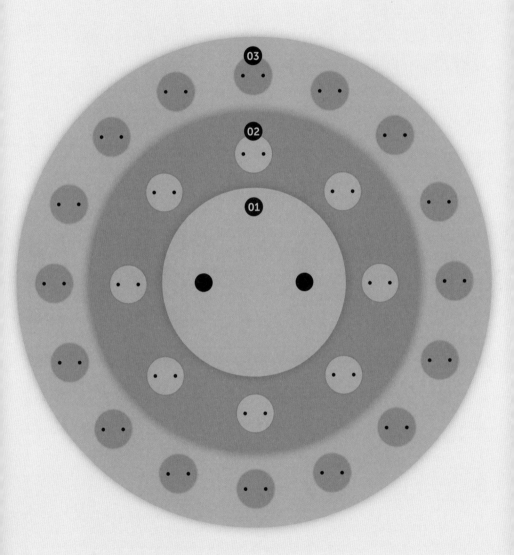

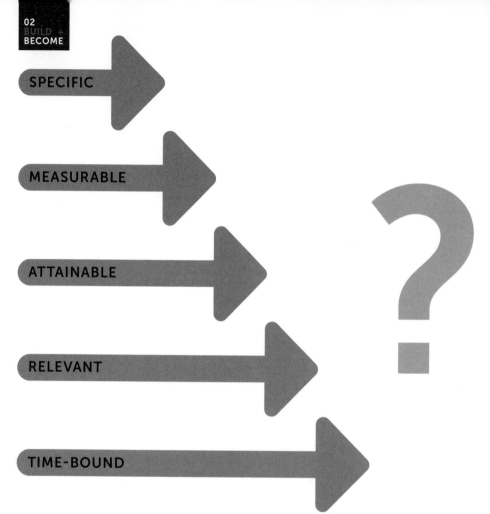

SPECIFIC

MEASURABLE

ATTAINABLE

RELEVANT

TIME-BOUND

?

BE SMART

As ambitions move into the world they must be stated clearly and broken down into their constituent parts. Goals become projects, actions, tasks and processes. Daily practices and weekly or monthly check-ins enable us to stay on track, monitor progress and discover efficiencies and improvements. Check that you are giving yourself the best chance of meeting your goals by reviewing the following suggestions on goals and lists.

Goals Check-In

A goal is an expression of your intention and a sacred commitment to expend energy towards a valued aim. As you step into the vision for your life you will necessarily work towards multiple goals, large and small. Yet even when we know exactly what SMART goals are, we often forget to put the theory to work, failing to check in with our goals regularly and ensure they meet the SMART criteria. If you have not done this recently, I encourage you to do it now.

+ EXERCISE

Make a list of your current goals and check that they measure up to the SMART criteria. Reword them as necessary and remember to hold yourself accountable by diarizing a weekly or monthly Goals Check-in on your calendar.

DO
Tasks that you will realistically complete today.

DOING
Larger tasks/projects that you are working on but will not complete today.

Renovating my van

Building my future business

Lists

I used to create an unrealistic to-do list at the beginning of every day, work my way through it as best I could, inevitably ending up with a stack of unfinished items to be transferred to tomorrow. The equivalent feeling would be that of an explorer attempting to summit a mountain, and no matter how far they climb, repeatedly reaching basecamp at the end of each day. Pretty demoralizing.

So instead of setting yourself up for a daily dose of disappointment, upgrade your to-do list by recording four task categories instead of one.

At the end of the day you will have a much more realistic sense of what you actually achieved, particularly as your DONE list might surprise you. Remember to always start a fresh list each day so you are not transferring yesterday's energy into tomorrow.

NOT DOING
Tasks or projects that you want to keep at the forefront of your mind although you are not working on them today.

Building a coffee & food trailer

DONE
Tasks that you completed today that were not on any of your lists.

NOW TAKE AMBITIONS TRANSLATE DAILY ACT

YOUR
AND
THEM INTO
ONS.

YOUR WORD

Your life is founded on multiple agreements and contracts that you have given your word to. In some ways this may feel surprising, simply because we tend not to think about life in these terms. You give your word when you sign a contract or make an agreement whether it is spoken or recorded in writing. Some of these are external agreements with others, such as a job contract, and some are internal agreements with yourself, to always do your best, or to look after your mother. Whatever you have given your word to unfolds into your experience of life itself.

Your word allows you to make sense of your identity and the circumstances of your life through narrative and relationships. You use your word to make requests, to commune with others, to be part of something, to lead and to inspire. Your word is primary, so it is important to make it count.

In the paradigm of Conscious Leadership your word counts when it is imbued with clarity and arises from the space beyond fear. When words are expressed with pristine clarity they are potent. When words arise from a fearless space, they are authentic and connected. When the two come together, something new is born and the world shifts.

Conversely, when fear is present and clarity absent, your word results in chaos, drama and broken promises.

Because many of your internal agreements were made in the past, perhaps even in childhood, you may not be aware of them all. It is therefore worthwhile welcoming them back into view and reviewing them periodically to ensure they feel current and authentic.

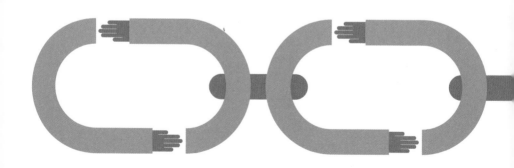

✚ EXERCISE

STAGE 1

Make a list of your current contracts and agreements.

Contracts

Work contracts, marriage contract, finance contracts...

External Agreements

Relationship agreements, community agreements, family agreements...

Internal Agreements

I promise myself I will be/do...

STAGE 2

Before you review your agreements, take a moment to read and sit with this list of 'The Top 5 Regrets of The Dying' by Bronnie Ware:

01. I wish I'd had the courage to live a life true to myself, not the life others expected of me.

02. I wish I hadn't worked so hard.

03. I wish I'd had the courage to express my feelings.

04. I wish I had stayed in touch with my friends.

05. I wish that I had let myself be happier.

STAGE 3

Finally, as you review your list, consider if everything you have given your word to feels aligned, balanced and in line with your values. If you feel an urge to change, release or add further contracts, do so with care, or make a note to return to the exercise to reflect further.

THE POWER OF CLARITY

An excellent way of aligning your word with your vision, values and goals is to tune in every morning to your intentions by completing the sentence starters below.

As a practice, this works best if you give yourself a few moments to drop in to the present moment on the breath and then read each statement, allowing your answers to be spontaneous and authentic. If you wish to write them down in your notes instead of saying them aloud, this works just as well, and creates a growing record of your intentions.

As you repeat the exercise daily, you may find that what you say or write surprises you. This is perfectly normal. Sometimes spontaneity taps you into wisdom and sometimes into the meaningless. Trust what comes and notice how your answers evolve over the days and weeks.

01. Today I am committed to:
02. Today I will make my contribution by:
03. Today I am most grateful for:
04. Today I let go of:
05. Today I forgive:

Morning Ritual
Your Morning Ritual is a microcosm of your life. It includes all the things you do between waking and leaving the house or getting into your day: showering, brushing teeth, eating, drinking, dressing, and so on.

When I wake up I go through my morning practice, which includes breath awareness, stretching, strengthening, meditation and intentions. This ritual allows me to tune into myself and the new energy present at the start of the day, as well as allowing me to connect with my vision and values.

As you progress through the lessons I will be inviting you to consider adding extra elements to your current Morning Ritual. Not all of the suggestions may resonate, so experiment with the ones that spark interest, and record in your notebook the impact of each addition. By the end of the book you will have fine-tuned your own ritual.

PRACTICE
In order to make space for new elements in your Morning Ritual, I am going to start by setting you a seven-day challenge to not look at your smart device for thirty minutes after waking. If the research is right, you will start to notice a greater sense of positivity and feel less stressed. Continue the practice if you notice benefits in your mental clarity and sense of wellbeing.

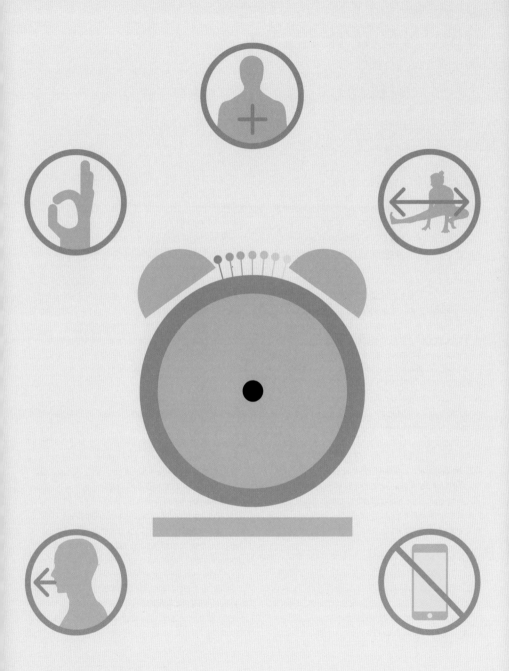

BOUNDARIES

A single word can change the direction of history: Yes. No. Stop. Wait. Go.

While the theory of boundaries is simple, the practice of expressing and enforcing them clearly and compassionately is not. Clear boundaries allow you to move through your day with peaceful ease. Weak boundaries engender resentment, overwhelm and leave you feeling like a victim of your circumstances.

Primary to being able to express boundaries well is clarity on what is and is not ok with you. This is deeply personal and may require serious reflection. Because many of us have been socialized as people-pleasers, it can be difficult to know what your authentic preferences are. If you find yourself answering most questions with *I don't mind*, spend a little time each day giving yourself permission to tune into, and speak up for, your preferences. Start with small things and build from there. It is not about being selfish, it is about being self-aware.

How To Say No

The art of Conscious Leadership is saying *yes* and meaning it wholeheartedly, and saying *no* while staying connected.

When I was about to begin my traineeship as a pupil Barrister (effectively a year-long interview), an older friend advised me to occasionally say no when being asked to do something by the clerks. Although terrifying, I put it into practice on a number of occasions and always made sure I gave good reasons. I learned early on that being able to say no actually engenders respect.

By saying yes to numerous things, people find themselves over-committed and overwhelmed. This often stems from the misconception that saying *no* is a rejection of the person asking. Remember it is absolutely possible to say no to a task or agreement, while also staying connected to the person and even strengthening the relationship. Byron Katie, prolific author and founder of The Work, talks about the 'Loving No'. It is a way of imbuing your *no* with kindness, compassion and an intention to continue relating.

If you sense that your no might be misconstrued, say it in person or pick up the phone. You may be able to offer an explanation, regrets or an alternative, and your spoken words are less likely to be misunderstood. Above all, remember that it is a kindness to all involved that you only commit yourself when you wholeheartedly mean it.

SHADOW WORK

One does not become enlightened by imagining figures of light, but by making the darkness conscious.
Carl Jung

To do justice to our exploration of self-knowledge it is vital to consider that the self is made up of both darkness and light. Your shadow, then, is made up of undesirable and repressed aspects of self – all the things you may dislike, feel unable to accept, or may be unable to see. When people point out your shadow qualities, you may feel disturbed, shame or a profound sense of unfairness.

To give an example, my shadow self is arrogant, ruthless, rude, angry, sullen and believes that life is futile. Learning to embrace these difficult truths, rather than fear them, was not easy, but has allowed me to experience myself more authentically, and has given me greater peace and wholeness.

In bringing the shadow into the light of awareness, you replace the denial of unwanted and unacceptable parts with a compassionate acceptance of personal truth. The shadow loses its power over you, and can find a peaceful place of integration. Here we are working with boundaries in a very different way. By noticing and accepting contradictory aspects of our nature it is possible to embrace them and in doing so allow them to transform and integrate.

Remember, you do not shine a light upon the shadow to give yourself another reason to beat yourself up. You do it to notice this natural aspect of your humanity and to practise compassion for yourself.

+ EXERCISE

Embracing the shadow is deep work
requiring courage and a stable foundation.
If you are not feeling healthy, strong and
centred today, leave this section for another
time, or come back to it with a trusted friend
or a professional.

List three negative qualities that have been
pointed out in you by others and which you
have trouble accepting.

01. _Jelously_
02. _Blunt_
03. _Selfish_

List three emotions that you find difficult to
express around others.

01. _Love_
02. _Vulnerability_
03. _Sadness_

List three triggers that provoke a defensive or
angry reaction.

01. _Someone talking about me_
02. _Feeling trapped_
03.

Now take a deep breath, look over the lists
you have made, and allow yourself to see
your challenges. Notice how each behaviour
has nuanced reasoning, patterns and habits
behind it. Offer yourself compassion for
doing your best in the circumstances of your
life and notice that we are all in some way
struggling. Notice also that you are ok.

TOOLKIT

01

At the start of your Conscious Leadership exploration it is important to take the time to develop a vision of yourself and the future you are stepping into. As you step forward into that vision, the path ahead will be rich with complex decisions. Naming your values and holding them close will offer you consistency, clarity and direction when it comes to choosing your next move.

02

Every ambition you ever achieved was made up of a multitude of tiny practical actions that built one by one towards an aspirational destination. These small actions make up the terrain of our daily lives. Over time, instead of working harder and longer hours, learn to work smarter and more efficiently by utilizing goals, lists and schedules to plan your way forward.

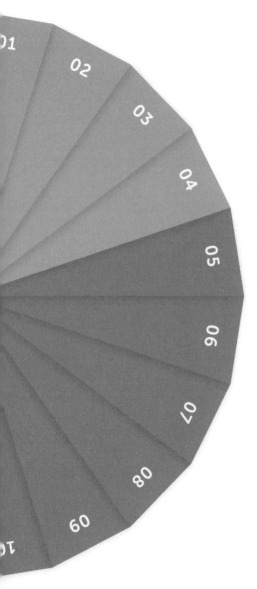

03

Communication is the foundation of all human endeavour. What you give your word to by way of contracts and agreements will turn into your lived experience. Clarity and precision are paramount. Your word is primary, so align it with your values and intentions and make it count.

04

Saying *yes* is easy, but finding the ability to say *no* is not. Leaning into clear boundaries becomes essential if you seek to lead with consistency, compassion and integrity. Understanding all aspects of your character helps you live with clarity and courage. You have already looked under the darkest rocks, so you have nothing to fear.

FURTHER LEARNING

READ

Conscious Business: How to Build Value Through Values
Fred Kofman (Sounds True Inc.; reprint edition, 2014)

The Integral Vision: A Very Short Introduction to the Revolutionary Integral Approach to Life, God, the Universe, and Everything
Ken Wilber (Shambhala Publications Inc., 2007)

The Miracle Morning: The 6 Habits That Will Transform Your Life Before 8AM
Hal Elrod (John Murray Learning, 2017)

Loving What Is: Four Questions That Can Change Your Life
Byron Katie and Stephen Mitchell (Rider; first paperback edition, 2002)

Find Your Why: A Practical Guide for Discovering Purpose for You and Your Team
Simon Sinek, David Mead, et al (Portfolio Penguin, 2017)

DOWNLOAD

The Work App by Byron Katie leads you through the process of her four questions, which are designed to free you from negative thinking and suffering. Watch some of Katie's videos first to get a sense of the process.

LISTEN

If you would like to take your exploration of the shadow further, listen to the audiobook *Knowing Your Shadow: Becoming Intimate With All that You Are* by Robert Augustus Masters PhD (Sounds True Inc., 2013).

INVESTIGATE

In addition to upgrading your own digital behaviours, parents may also be looking for ways to set appropriate limits on the use of digital devices by their children. There are great products on the market to help with this now: just search 'internet parental control device'.

SELF-MAINTENANCE

LESSONS

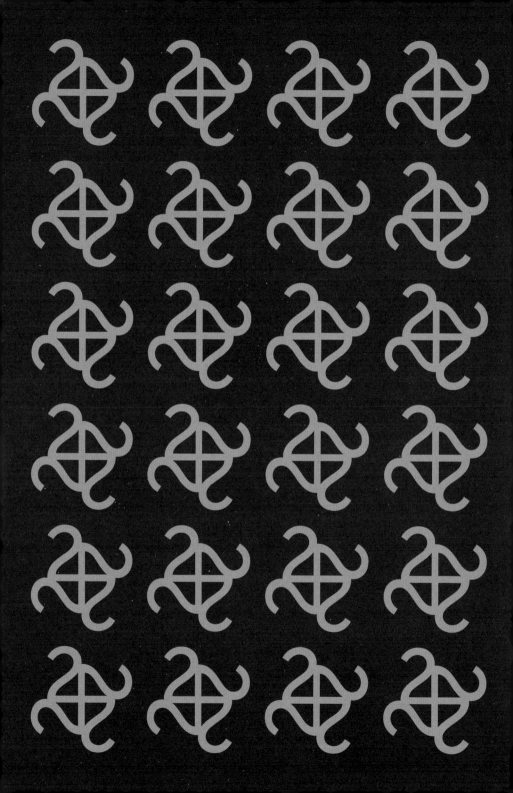

While we draw on others for support and care, we take individual responsibility for leading our own wellbeing journey.

Being a Conscious Leader means taking care of your instrument: your body, your mind, your energy, your state of being.

When I began studying with my current meditation teacher in 2008 I was somewhat surprised that for the first three years, our focus kept returning to Self-Maintenance, which at the time seemed self-indulgent to me, and a little selfish. One of the first suggestions that she offered was that I start weight training in order to become more grounded and embodied. This wasn't what I expected, but I went along with it, and she then led me through a process that helped me discover the finer details of what my body, mind and being needed to thrive.

As the years went on, and I became stronger, healthier and more centred, I noticed that my capacity to sit in stillness with awareness was also growing. My ability to navigate the complexities of my life increased, and I started to get a sense of what many teachers point to when they describe the capacity to demonstrate equanimity throughout the course of events. I learned that my own wellbeing was foundational to both excellence and the quality of anything I wished to contribute at home and at work.

The truth is that being a human being is a high-maintenance occupation. Whether studied meditation is for you or not, the lesson here is about the benefits of recognizing and actively drawing on your own resources. If you want to know your best health, strength, resilience and happiness, it is important to accept that it takes planning, commitment and consistency.

While we draw on others for support and care, we take individual responsibility for leading our own wellbeing journey. The aim of the Conscious Leader is to look after themselves so completely, that when they walk in the room, they are fully resourced, energized and creative. Others feel their vitality and dynamism, and they inspire outcomes previously out of reach.

To get a sense of this, imagine that later today you were to walk in to a meeting feeling great, only to find a serious argument in full flow. How skilled do you think you would be at leading the energy in the room from conflict to calm? Alternatively, how quickly might you lose your sense of positivity and instead resonate with the conflict. In other words, how well can you retain your own shape, and how often do you bend to the shape of others? In this chapter we will look at how to build your resources so that you can hold your own whatever your day throws at you.

SUPPORT TEAM

You cannot do it all by yourself. Anyone on a mission needs a serious support team.

If you were an Olympic athlete you would have an elite team working tirelessly to keep you at your best. There would be a trainer, nutritionist, sports psychologist, masseur, physiotherapist, doctors, and many more.

Now consider that you too have high expectations of yourself, in your career, as a parent, as a leader, or in other ways.

In the paradigm of Conscious Leadership, health and strength are foundational to excellence. Far from being a selfish preoccupation, ensuring that you have taken care of your wellbeing needs allows you to feel fully resourced. In turn this increases your capacity to be of service to family, friends and at work. Having a few select individuals, whether it be a coach, masseur, yoga teacher or career mentor, who assist you with your wellbeing and/or performance, is simply good practice when it comes to stepping into your full potential.

It is easy to forget the people who are already part of your support network. Family members, partners, best friends, colleagues and pets might also be part of your team. Reflecting on where you currently find support and considering whether you need more, are important questions that are better asked sooner rather than later. Counter-intuitively, the time to invest in your wellbeing is when you are well. Wellbeing then becomes a habit and a resource that can be drawn on when challenges arise.

+ EXERCISE

Who is on your support team? Make a list and if it looks or feels a little empty, consider who you would place on your recruit list? Would you benefit from a life coach, therapist, personal trainer, virtual assistant, a cleaner or someone else? Take recommendations from trusted friends and make time for your personal wellbeing.

SUPPORT TEAM	RECRUIT LIST

WELLBEING

Your body is the vehicle of your consciousness. It is resourceful, creative, flexible and powerful, yet it cannot thrive without your willing collaboration and care. This means that the key player in your support team is of course *you*. You are the leader, the planner, the participant, the one that shows up for class, session or practice.

In becoming the mindful caretaker of your body, you reflect to others the depth of your caring, and your capacity for wholeness. When you walk in the room your body speaks before you do. What is it saying? What do others know about you before you open your mouth?

This is not about aesthetics, muscles or the perfect body, it is about what emanates from your physical form as a primary vibration. When you are connected to the body, that is leadership, and it's contagious.

Being a leader can no longer mean shunning the physical body and allowing it to play second fiddle to your busy-ness, your business or your importance.

A Conscious Leader prioritizes self-care and then reflects the same respect and caring to those around them.

Seasonal Plan

The mind and body respond to seasonal changes and enjoy variety when it comes to nutrition and exercise. The seasons are therefore a very useful and natural prompt for you to consider the focus of your activities. A balanced wellbeing plan will include inspiring foods and activities that help maintain your health, stamina, flexibility and strength throughout the year. Keep in mind the time-honoured principles of *like increases like* and *opposites balance* taken from Ayurvedic practice. This is why cooling foods and activities are great in the summer, and warming ones in the winter. Simple.

Look over the Seasonal Wellbeing diagram opposite, reflect on your current goals and consider if there are any changes you wish to make to your routine. Return to this section when the seasons change.

MORNING RITUAL

It is extremely empowering to insert a daily dose of fitness into your Morning Ritual. I call this your 'Better Than Nothing Workout' because it is super-easy to complete. It is quick, requires no equipment and ensures you get moving at the start of each day.

Choose three exercises you already know well, do ten reps of each and you are done.

BETTER THAN NOTHING WORKOUT

EXERCISES

10 Push-ups ☐

10 Sit-ups ☐

10 Squats ☐

WINTER

FOCUS: Immune support / less is more.

EXERCISE GOAL: Stamina and strength. Workouts to warm the body and build capacity.

EAT: Hearty hot foods.

DRINK: Herbal teas.

SPRING

FOCUS: Reset / renew.

EXERCISE GOAL: Cleanse and lighten. Join a new class or group.

EAT: Light foods, lots of fresh fruit and vegetables.

DRINK: Water and fresh green juices.

AUTUMN

FOCUS: Grounding / simplifying.

EXERCISE GOAL: Stamina and stress release. Introduce restorative, tension-releasing aspects to your workout.

EAT: Soups and warming spices.

DRINK: Warm water and teas.

SUMMER

FOCUS: Fun / community / adventure.

EXERCISE GOAL: Flexibility. Moderate workouts during cooler hours.

EAT: Cooling foods with high water content, salads.

DRINK: Lots of water to stay hydrated.

MIND

Using Awareness

Philosophers, scientists and psychologists have argued for centuries over the simple yet profound question: what is mind? For me, the simplest and most useful definition is this: 'mind is awareness'. And awareness is incredibly powerful.

Close your eyes for a moment and try to find the edge of your awareness...

Your awareness (the mind) is infinitely expansive and not limited to the local brain. I am going to guess therefore that you weren't able to find the edge of your awareness.

Awareness is at the heart of being conscious, so when it comes to leadership, awareness is everything. The more aware you can be of yourself, others and the salient facts, the better chance you have of making the right next move. Yet to connect to the full potential of your awareness, the mind must be accessed in the right way. The route of access is as follows:

01. Embodiment – body online
02. Connectivity – heart online
03. Mind – wisdom online

Most have never been taught this route, and instead go straight to Mind without stages one and two. When the mind comes on in this way, it may sound intelligent but is frequently disconnected, fearful and limited. This highly destructive mindset translates into unwise or uncaring decisions, short-termism and limited solutions.

The good news is that more and more people every day are learning through simple practices how to show up with their resources fully online. Here's how you can ensure that you do, too.

+ EXERCISE

In this thought experiment, the aim is to explore the difference between bringing worried and calm attention to a current challenge.

WORRIED ATTENTION
01. Bring to mind a current challenge.
02. Set a timer for 45 seconds and worry about it until the alarm sounds.
03. Note the outcome.

Stay with the same challenge and follow these steps.

CALM ATTENTION
01. Breathe in for five seconds and out for five seconds.
02. Feel your feet on the floor.
03. Notice the weight of your body.
04. Breathe into and through the whole body.
05. Remember all your body parts; allow the mind to inhabit the body.

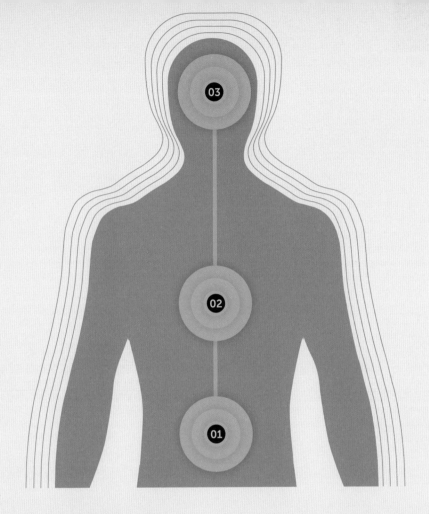

06. Bring your awareness to the heart. Notice its movement and rhythm.

07. Breath in for five seconds and out for five seconds.

08. Set a timer and now bring your focus to your challenge for 45 seconds.

09. Note the outcome.

Although this process may feel cumbersome the first few times you try it, stick with it. Being a Conscious Leader requires a regular practice of traversing from fear response to wise response. As you begin to notice that the mind is more inspired, resourceful and creative when you are connected to the resources of the body, you will also notice your impact on others and on situations changing. You will be plugged in to infinite mind, where harmonic solutions, serendipity and right actions emerge. In this space, idea-generation and problem-solving become effortless.

NEGATIVITY BIAS

Ever noticed that your brain is far more eagerly preoccupied with your problems than all of the other wonderful things that happened in your day? This is not because there is something wrong with you, but because the human brain evolved with the primary motive of survival. This means that when nice things happen, they don't get much airtime because you are probably also safe when they happen, and the brain is optimized to keep you alert to danger. In the words of happiness expert Rick Hanson, the brain is 'Teflon for the positive and Velcro for the negative'.

In Stone Age times, if you saw a shape behind the trees, it was far more important that you assumed it was a lion and took evasive action, than hoped it was a rock and possibly met your end. Back then, people encountered mortal danger much more frequently, while in modern times, for most of us it is thankfully rare.

Yet the modern outcomes for the brain's negativity bias are two unhealthy preoccupations of mind: catastrophizing and rumination.

In these processes, the mind is either fast-forwarding to the future (catastrophizing) or mulling over the past (rumination), yet the body and your nervous system re-experiences the stress as if it was happening over and over in the present. The body does not know the difference between an imagined event, a remembered event and a real event.

This is as exhausting as it is futile. Remember the illuminating words of Mark Twain who points to this when he says: 'I've lived through some terrible things in my life, some of which actually happened'.

If any of this rings true for you and you would like to try something new, here is a simple, speedy exercise that can bring back some perspective and balance.

CATASTROPHIZING

That meeting went terribly. James really reacted badly. Agh – that look – he's going to complain to my boss. I'm going to come in tomorrow and be fired. What about the school fees? We'll have to move. I've let everyone down. I'm a failure.

RUMINATION

That meeting was a nightmare. I wish I'd said something else. Anything else. Why would I say that? It's so unlike me. That meeting will be the end of me. I've got to get myself out of this – how could I have been so silly? Why did I say that!? Eugh.

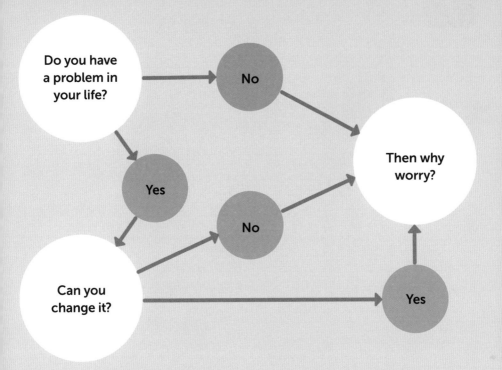

+ EXERCISE

On a piece of paper, draw a line down the middle to create two columns. Head the first column 'VENT' and the second column 'TRUE'. In the VENT column write down an unfiltered stream of consciousness:

VENT
I can't do it. I'm not clever enough.
I don't know what I'm doing. I'm lazy.
It is hopeless...

In the TRUE column, write down a list of facts that relate to the situation. Watch out for any assumptions, speculations or exaggerations. Only known facts are allowed:

TRUE
I am trying my best. This is a complex issue.
I can ask for support. I don't have all the information I need. I am working hard...

Now read both columns and write down three next steps:

NEXT STEPS
01. Tell Manager what happened.
02. Be open and honest.
03. Make amends with James.

WHEN YOU
CONNECTED
BODY THAT
LEADERSHIP
CONTAGIOU

ARE
TO THE
IS
AND IT'S
S.

ENERGY

Scenario 1

You are walking the dog after a long day at work. You're tired, and as you walk you try to catch up with emails on your phone. Distracted, you don't notice the pile of sweets at the side of the pavement. The dog wolfs them down. As you arrive home, the dog climbs on the sofa and vomits. You try not to but you can't help shouting at the dog. You spend an hour trying to clean the upholstery and eventually get into bed exhausted, but the dog wakes you up twice with further bouts of sickness. You wake up grumpy and tired and arrive at work bleary eyed. The first meeting of the day is a stonker. By 9.30am you barely feel human.

Scenario 2

You are walking the dog, enjoying the evening air. Your phone is at home as you want to maximize bonding time with your pet and enjoy the walk. Your alert presence allows you to steer the dog away from a pile of sweets. You return home feeling peaceful and connected. You get a good night's sleep and arrive at the office, where the first meeting is challenging. You navigate a tricky situation well and everyone leaves feeling motivated. You get into the rest of your day.

Perhaps the above scenarios resonate with you? How easy it is to fall into the trap of splitting attention between multiple

tasks, ending up doing them all less well, leading to a chain reaction of exhausting circumstances. The alternative is to be present in what you are doing, on task and alert. When we are able to do this we are efficiently using our energy and competently inhabiting our reality.

The Teaching of Done

The human spirit is boundless, eternal and infinite and this can lead to attitudes such as *'keep moving-keep pushing'* and *'pain is just weakness leaving the body'*. Yet the human body is limited, temporal and finite, and while your spirit never tires, your body does. It requires rest, nourishment and rejuvenation. More than that, it gently requests your listening.

At the beginning of the day your jug of energy is full. You can pour it into anything you like and it will magically refill overnight. You can do it all – you just can't do it all at the same time, on the same day, as at a certain point you will be *done*.

As with many truths, *The Teaching of Done* is both simple and obvious: when you are done, you are done. The body will quietly tell you when. Yet how often do you ignore it and push on? Being aware of this, noticing what happens when you do and when you don't, will help you to calibrate your task-load with your energy.

PRESSURE AND PERFORMANCE

When it comes to energy it is important to keep in mind the relationship between pressure and performance. You may have seen a version of The Pressure/Performance Scale opposite, which teaches that you need a certain amount of pressure to feel motivated and engaged in your activities; minimal pressure equates to boredom and inactivity. While it can be good to have periods where you are resting in the Comfort zone, it is also beneficial to be in the Stretch zone occasionally as your capacity for excellence increases here, even as the pressure mounts.

Problems come when you spend excessive time in the Strain zone, as this is where your ability to perform begins to decrease, and if the pressure increases further you are headed into the Fantasy zone, which is where both performance and health are likely to significantly suffer. Those who live in Strain and Fantasy are likely headed for burnout.

Questions
- Consider where you spend most of your time on the Pressure/ Performance Scale?
- Is your current energy spend sustainable?
- Are your energy habits in order?
- If rebalancing is necessary, what choices will you need to review?

BALANCING SPEND AND RESTORE
Part of managing your daily quota of energy is ensuring that you have the right balance between activities that spend your energy and those that restore it. Spend activities are those where you are left with less energy, such as work, childcare, scrolling through social media, worrying, and so on. Restore activities are those where you are left refreshed or with more energy, such as sleep, meditation, yoga, spending time with good friends or in nature, and so on. Consider too that some people you hang out with require more of your energy (spend), while others will leave you buoyant and energized (restore). Some will find going for a run a massive spend, for others it will be a refreshing restore. Becoming clear on the impact of your activities on your energy is an important step in navigating a sustainable balance.

PRESSURE/PERFORMANCE SCALE

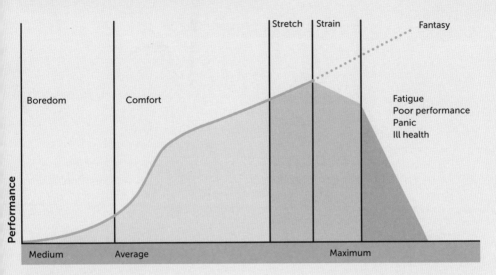

Performance

Boredom   Comfort   Stretch | Strain   Fantasy

Fatigue
Poor performance
Panic
Ill health

Medium   Average   Maximum

Level of pressure

✚ EXERCISE

Based on the last 24 hours, make a list of all your activities, allocating them to either the Spend or Restore column. Underline the Restore activities that happen more than three times a week. What three small changes could you have made to better manage your energy?

Spend	Restore

Three small changes

01.
02.
03.

WHAT IS EMBODIMENT?

In a collection of short stories called *Dubliners*, James Joyce started one ('A Painful Case') with the line, 'Mr. Duffy lived a short distance from his body'. With just nine words, Joyce captured one of the most disturbing consequences of the modern age: disembodiment – the sense of separation and disconnection many feel from the physical body.

Yet embodiment is key to performance. When a sprinter warms up, they bring awareness into the body, activating their limbs ready for the intense action ahead. When they step down into the starting blocks, they aim to connect body and mind so completely that when the starting gun fires, the legs and feet react instinctively and they experience an almost transcendent feeling of embodied presence as mind and body merge into one.

Embodiment then is consciously inhabiting the body and experiencing and processing reality through it. Yet when embodiment is weak you begin to think of yourself as a brain on legs and treat the physical body as little more than an inconvenience that moves you from place to place. This is why the most prolific mindfulness exercise is the Body Scan, which invites the warmth of awareness in stages through the body from feet to head. This exercise is often quite challenging for beginners, who may not have travelled through the wilderness of the body in this way before. One of the most natural things to discover in early practice is that a lot of the body feels empty, void or numb.

While it can feel quite bizarre to even try embodiment practices, you should explore and persevere so that you can connect with the full capabilities of the human body. For leadership is not conscious unless it is also embodied.

LANGUAGE OF EMBODIMENT

Understanding the language of embodiment can be very helpful as you learn to inhabit more of your body and experience.

INTEROCEPTION is your perception of what is occurring inside the body. The sensations found within can be subtle, nebulous, challenging, painful, persistent and/or fleeting.

PROPRIOCEPTION is your perception of where your body is in space relative to objects and people. You use it to find your seat in the cinema, to navigate a crowded room or to dribble around the opposition in basketball.

EXTERIOCEPTION describes what is happening outside of you; you might be working on a spreadsheet, watching a movie or listening to an audiobook.

Our focus in this lesson is on increasing INTEROCEPTION.

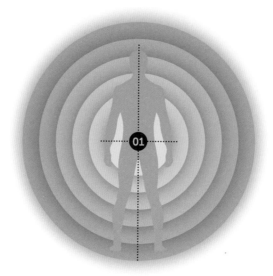

PRACTICE MAKES PEACEFUL

The following practices explore embodiment experientially. Centring Practice will prepare you to be at your best in important and challenging scenarios. You may wish to use it in advance of your next presentation, performance review or stakeholder meeting.

The Body Scan is a practice that many find calming, allowing you to pay attention to and reflect upon information within the body that often goes unnoticed (sensations, images, feelings and thoughts). Often practised in the evening, the Body Scan allows you to integrate the experience of your day in a different, and perhaps new, way.

PRACTICE 1: CENTRING

This is a simple yet powerful embodiment practice that you can do any time you need to bring yourself back to centre. It is inspired by the work of Embodied Leadership expert Richard Strozzi-Heckler. The first few times you practise it, take your time. You will be able to do it more quickly once it feels familiar. I like to do this practice before going to a meeting or delivering a talk. It brings all of my resources online and catalyzes clarity.

01. Weight Stand up and feel the weight of the body and the force of gravity connecting you to the Earth.

02. Length Centre yourself in length. Notice your full height from head to toe. Bring your awareness into the length of the body. You may perceive a sensation of growing taller, and the spine coming into a natural alignment.

03. Width Centre yourself in width. Notice your full width from left side to right side. Width symbolizes how you take up space. Inhabit the expanse of your width.

04. Depth Centre yourself in depth from the front body to the back body. Depth brings in the notion of time. Notice all of

your past moments, teachers, ancestors and experiences behind you. Notice all of your unknown future moments and expansive potential ahead of you.

05. Intention Centre yourself in your intention. What is your intention in this moment?

PRACTICE 2: THE BODY SCAN

Remember that your most natural state is embodiment and you are only looking for sensations that are already there. An experience of numbness, or absence of sensation, is as worthy of note as anything else. With repetition, your sensitivity to the tides and weather of internal sensation may increase.

01. Sit or lie down comfortably.

02. Start by bringing awareness to the feet and toes. What sensations are present here? If you wish, curl the toes and then release them. What can you feel?

03. Take several breaths.

04. At your own pace, work your way up the body, feeling for sensation at each location and tensing and releasing if you wish: shins, knees, thighs, pelvis, abdomen, chest, back, arms, hands, neck, head, scalp. Take your time, and pause to take several breaths before moving on.

05. When you have been through the scan, take three conscious breaths into the whole body.

06. With an intention of present moment awareness, see if you can notice the union of mind and body.

As you emerge from the practice, draw a simple outline of your body in your notes, if you wish, and use words, shading and your own creativity to record what you experienced.

BUILD +
BECOME

TOOLKIT

05

We place high demands on our incredible bodies while sometimes forgetting to invest in our health, strength and wellbeing. The Conscious Leader does not take their body for granted but cares for it so they can present the best version of themselves to the world.

06

Becoming adept at navigating the terrain of the mind is crucial for those that lead. The fascinating exploration of mind and awareness brings us face to face with our worries, negativity bias and worst-case scenarios, but also allows us to utilize the mind to achieve our maximum potential.

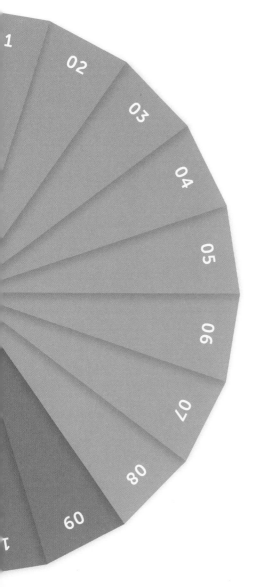

07

Maintaining presence and managing your daily quota of energy to take account of short-term tasks, medium-term goals and lifelong health is quite the conundrum. Know when you are done and keep yourself in balance by understanding which activities spend and restore your energy. You *can* do it all – just not all in one day.

08

Embodiment is the skill of holding the human body with awareness as you navigate your day. When you are embodied, you are connected to your internal data resources and you feel centred in your intentions, actions and communications. Embodiment is supported by simple practices such as Centring and the Body Scan.

FURTHER LEARNING

READ

4 Pillar Plan: How to Relax, Eat, Move and Sleep Your Way to a Longer, Healthier Life
Dr Rangan Chatterjee (Penguin Life, 2017)

Your Brain at Work: Strategies for Overcoming Distraction, Regaining Focus, and Working Smarter All Day Long
David Rock (Harper Business, 2009)

Thrive: The Third Metric to Redefining Success and Creating a Happier Life
Arianna Huffington (WH Allen, 2015)

TRY

Gabrielle Roth's **5Rhythms** is a dynamic movement practice that ignites creativity, connection and community. Classes are taught all over the world; find your local class online at www.5rhythms.com

The **Sleepio App** is a digital cognitive behavioural therapy (CBT) program that aims to help you sleep well naturally.

LISTEN

The **Insight Timer App** offers a multitude of free guided meditations, including a huge variety of Body Scan variations, including some by the author.

TRAIN

Learn more about Embodied Leadership on a course, such as those at the Strozzi Institute in Northern California: www.strozziinstitute.com

Begin or deepen your yoga journey with a class at one of **triyoga**'s beautiful spaces throughout London: www.triyoga.co.uk Or check the internet to find a yoga class local to you.

SELF-MANAGEMENT

LESSONS

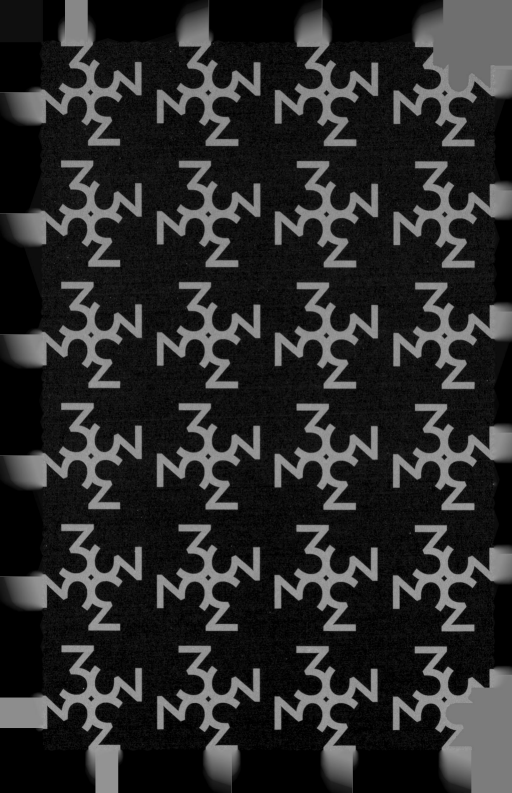

As you develop increased self-management skills, you will be able to remain calm and stable in the face of challenging words, thoughts and actions.

As a leader, all eyes are on you as you navigate the challenges of the day, whether at work or at home. How well you are able to navigate from fear to calm, from worry to resourcefulness, and from conflict to resolution (especially when you are in the spotlight) determines how effective you can be as a leader.

It is in these conflict-ridden moments that real leadership either shows up or evaporates. It is also where your vision, values, goals and intentions are tested.

In psychology, the window of tolerance describes the zone of arousal (physical and mental alertness) in which an individual is able to function well. This concept helps us to bring awareness to the range of circumstances and situations that commonly arise in life through which you can remain stable, calm and effective, as well as to other events that destabilize you, pushing you beyond this window.

When it comes to self-management, Conscious Leaders seek practical ways of increasing the size of their window of tolerance in order to better deal with the challenges of high-pressure environments. After all, others look to you when the proverbial hits the fan, when change is announced and when the tough decisions have to be called. They might hope that out of everyone in the room, you have the greatest capacity for stability in tough times.

This then is the skill of navigating shifting sands and modelling mature, honest self-regulation. This is something that you can pass on to others just by practising it yourself, and something that people sense about you before you even say a word.

If this is a growth area for you, welcome to the club. Rest assured that you are in good company and that mindfulness as well as other tools can be a key support. Mindfulness teaches you how to feel safer within the difficult internal spaces of fear, panic, worry, chaos and confusion. Over time it may allow you to open your window of tolerance a little wider.

As you develop increased self-management skills, you will be able to remain calm and stable in the face of challenging words, thoughts and actions.

STRESS RESILIENCE

If there was a magic button that could make all of the stresses in your life disappear, would you press it?

Stanford Health Psychologist Kelly McGonigal says: 'Stress arises when something you care about is at stake'. Let that sink in for a second, then reconsider the above question.

Before you answer, think about what else would have to disappear for your life to actually be stress-free? If you normally stress about your child, parents or pet, your ambitions, hopes and dreams, the magic button may well erase them. In fact, under McGonigal's definition, the opposite of stress would not be joy, happiness and tranquillity, but apathy, as your life reduces to a bleak existence in which there is nothing to care about.

As a reframing of stress, I find this definition a powerful alternative to the usual negative messages that abound. It reminds me that a life lived well will include caring about a multitude of things that are deeply precious, and that the price of this caring is a share of stress. It is not possible to have one without the other.

This then opens the door to attending to the stressors of life with a little more aptitude and compassion. Instead of trying to erase stress, how about seeking a new perspective on it, and dare I say locating a sense of appreciation for it?

Downloading your Stress Cloud
Most people live under a cloud of stress. The cloud is full of everything that you have not yet completed, all the grumbles at work and at home, your financial fears, health worries and the trials and tribulations of daily life.

One of the best ways to take stock of your current stress cloud is to list all of your stressors, to give yourself a moment to step back and see the reality of your current situation. The following exercise is inspired by the work of expert Fitness and Wellness Consultant, Kimberlee Bethany Bonura PhD.

+ EXERCISE

Note: The aim of this exercise is to give perspective rather than to be therapeutic. If you are in a period of trauma, you may find the following exercise upsetting. Go gently, seek support or skip ahead.

01. Read the key.
02. Allocate all current stressors, large and small, to the relevant quadrant.
03. Consider the questions below.

KEY:	
Trauma	**Hassles**
Life events causing serious distress and disturbance.	Work deadlines, low-level relationship issues, financial concerns. . .
Chores	**Irritants**
Daily domestic activities.	The blister on your heel, the ants at the picnic. . .

QUESTIONS:

01. **Having completed the exercise, do you feel more or less stressed?**
02. **Why do you think that is?**
03. **Do you have enough support to deal with what you are going through currently? If no, is there someone you can reach out to, or a new choice you can make?**
04. **As you look at your chart, is there anything to appreciate? For example, you may have noticed that your trauma quadrant is currently empty.**

While the exercise can leave some feeling more stressed and others lighter, the overall benefit is perspective. Taking a step back allows you to feel less identified with anxious, negative thoughts and creates space for making clear decisions and choosing wise actions.

THE GIFT OF PERSPECTIVE

With a little more perspective on your current situation, you can see more clearly what might be your next right move. If you are going through a traumatic period and have not yet sought help, you may feel inspired to do so. In times of trauma, we need to reach out and draw on the assistance of our support team. If feeling burdened by the hassles and chores of life, know that these are always going to be there to some degree. It is therefore important to develop a healthy mindset as the research shows that your approach to daily hassles is a more accurate predictor of anxiety and depression than the absence or presence of major traumas. Finally, if you are allowing irritants to weigh heavily, mindfulness teaches you how to let them go. Try the practice on page 126.

STOP

Amygdala Hijack

Imagine you are giving a presentation, updating senior staff on your team's progress and development plan for the next quarter. You have focused on recent wins, upcoming resource requirements and high-level future planning when your manager chimes in with, 'This isn't what we asked for. Where are the figures? What's the point of all these pretty slides when the detail is completely absent?'

Even though the last few slides have the numbers that your boss is looking for, the abrupt interruption and aggressive tone catalyzes a spike of anxiety that you experience physically as you notice your hands becoming sweaty, your face flushed and you struggle to find your words. This is amygdala hijack, and overcoming it requires self-regulation and stress-resilience – key skills of Conscious Leaders.

Your amygdala are two pea-sized structures in the brain that effectively operate as your alarm system. Activated when perceived danger is present, they set in motion a series of reactions that optimize your body and brain for survival. This includes diverting resources from your pre-frontal cortex (the PFC is responsible for rational thinking, decision-making and higher order brain functions) to supply the muscles and vital organs instead. This is an appropriate reaction when a tiger walks into the room, but not during a tricky presentation or when you are criticized by a stranger. In those situations, you need your PFC fully functioning to respond as your best self, and this is why it is vital to build self-awareness around your stress-reactivity, and to learn skills that can help you regulate it.

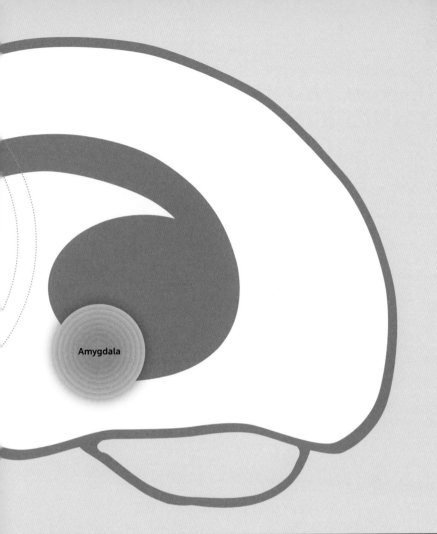

Amygdala

PRACTICE

STOP is a pocket-practice taught on Mindfulness Based Stress Reduction (MBSR) courses to help you regain clarity and calm during stressful situations.

When you notice that your amygdala has jumped into action, first ask yourself: *Am I in physical danger?*

If the answer is no, try this:

S – Stop and pause. Ground yourself by feeling the feet on the floor.

T – Take a conscious breath. Inhale with awareness, exhale and let go.

O – Observe what is happening internally and externally. Is there a new opportunity?

P – Proceed, or STOP again.

SURFING CHANGE
AND UNCERTAINTY

There are times in life when change and uncertainty increase. Divorce, redundancy, becoming a parent, moving home, starting a new job. . . While these are all very different life events, each requires you to stand firm as the ground you stand on shakes and moves.

Yet no matter how much they are disliked, change and uncertainty are not going away. In fact, paradoxically, they form some of the more reliable facets of the human experience. So, what would a healthy, practical approach to these tricky certainties of life look like? Proverbs abound that encapsulate the ancient wisdom here. Take this one for example:

You can't stop the waves, but you can learn to surf. (Unknown)

The advice here is not to place the anchor of your being (your centre) in the circumstances of your life but within yourself (your resourcefulness, your creativity, your skilfulness). The trick to surfing, after all, is not to find a ripple-free ocean, but to locate the point of stillness within yourself and enjoy the ride.

Life is a constant practice of being dislocated from your centre and finding your way back. Each time you fall off the board, you climb back on, a little wiser, more skilful, becoming adept. This internal mapping of your interior spaces and the courage to keep returning to centre is the path of Conscious Leadership.

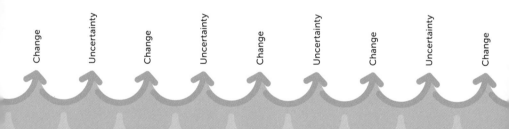

+ EXERCISE

The brain's negativity bias leads you to believe that any change from the status quo will be problematic. The following exercise seeks to challenge that idea and to demonstrate that there are in fact no wrong paths in life. All paths hold experience, learning and the potential for wisdom, particularly when approached with optimism.

01. Make a list of three significant changes that occurred in your past that you were extremely worried about but turned out to have unexpected benefits.

02. Make a list of three of your mistakes that taught you something important.

03. Reflect on one change that is occurring in your life right now that you might be resisting. Consider practically how you might soften your resistance and embrace this change, even though it is frightening?

Change

Uncertainty

Change

Uncertainty

Change

Uncertainty

Change

Uncertainty

Change

EMBRACING CHANGE

The process of transformation is not always beautiful or comfortable. Do you remember marvelling at the caterpillar who had no idea what it was going to become when it started to build its chrysalis, but went inside anyway? It was so fully committed to the unknown future that it was willing to abandon itself completely to the process. In fact, if you were to look at the pupae in the mid stages of metamorphosis, you would see a muddy digestive mess and could easily conclude that the caterpillar had met with disaster. But no, everything is exactly as it should be. The process is perfectly progressing, not even a millisecond could be skipped.

It just goes to show that during periods of change, at certain moments all may be in perfect order, yet look really ugly. Your trust in the process symbolizes a deeper acceptance of the progression of change, which becomes vital the more committed you are to your personal development and evolution.

At a certain point, a leader must break through acceptance and find their way to deeply welcome change and inspire its acceptance by others. A powerful example of this is captured in Deepak Chopra's affirmation: 'The more uncertain things seem to be, the more secure I will feel, because uncertainty is the path to my freedom'.

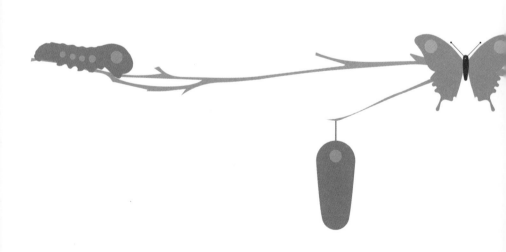

PRACTICE

Imagine that your employer has unexpectedly announced that it is merging with another firm and that you and your whole department will be made redundant. What positive steps could you take in response to this news?

01. ANCHOR YOURSELF
When everything feels like it is in flux, remember that there are stable aspects of life that can be appreciated at this time. It might be your partner, family, your book club, your fitness class, and so on. Keep investing time in these things.

02. ACCEPT WHERE YOU ARE
Even though it may be the hardest thing to do, start by accepting your current situation. Acceptance is the fulcrum of reality and precedes any worthwhile change.

03. SELF-CARE
Increasing self-care during change is crucial. Keep yourself grounded with good food, connect with old friends, book the massage you have been promising yourself.

04. INVEST IN YOUR SKILLS
Now is a great time to take advantage of any training courses that might be on offer, or even consider a relevant external program. Ensure your CV is up to date and represents who you have become. Rewrite your stock covering letter.

05. ONE FOOT IN FRONT OF THE OTHER
Change can be disorientating, and you cannot anticipate every outcome, so keep your trajectory clear by returning to this question: *What is my next right move?*

06. SLEEP ON IT
In times of change, when it comes to decision-making, slow things down. If you have made a big decision, sleep on it to check it stills feels right in the morning.

07. LISTEN
In a quiet moment, take a few calming breaths and reflect on the question: *As this change unfolds, what am I being called into?*

COMING HO
CENTRE IS
WORK OF C
LEADERSHP

ME TO
THE
ONSCIOUS
P .

EMOTIONAL INTELLIGENCE

Sue entered a macho workforce at twenty-one where she quickly learned that emotions equated to weakness, coldness to strength and utility to value. After an anxious first few years, she learned to ignore her emotions and subconsciously linked her value to the company with her ability to do this successfully. Now, at forty-two, Sue sometimes finds it hard to relate to others outside of work, and her partner criticizes her for being aloof and unfeeling.

This experience is not unusual; Sue's mindset is shared by many. The unfortunate consequence of this is that generations of workers learned to divorce themselves from their emotions as they entered the office. And in that denial of emotional awareness, they cut themselves off from the possibility of developing one of their most valuable resources: emotional intelligence.

Emotional intelligence (EQ) describes your capacity to identify, manage and work with your emotions, and those of others. Without understanding the validity and importance of emotions, the human animal is mercenary, disconnected and compassionless.

Having only been identified as an area of academic study in 1985, emotional intelligence and its application to leadership came later. In 1998 it was described by Daniel Goleman as follows:

...emotional intelligence is the sine qua non of leadership. Without it, a person can have the best training in the world, an incisive, analytical mind, and an endless supply of smart ideas, but he still won't make a great leader.

Since then, increasing EQ has become the number one goal of leadership training and, like any skill, it needs continual development to grow and harness its benefits.

Emotional intelligence as a differentiator
When you qualify for any job, your peers are likely to be as smart, or smarter, than you (having jumped the same IQ hurdles). So once you have your foot in the door, what determines who progresses, winning promotions into management and leadership roles? Emotional intelligence is the differentiator.

As you look over the skills of EQ in the Emotional Intelligence Framework opposite (adapted from that of leading expert Daniel Goleman), you will soon see why.

EMOTIONAL INTELLIGENCE FRAMEWORK

SELF-AWARENESS

- Emotional self-awareness.
- Accurate self-assessment.
- Self-confidence, self-compassion.

SELF-MANAGEMENT

- Emotional self-control, transparency, low stress reactivity.
- Adaptability, capable of self-leadership/initiative.
- Optimistic and achievement oriented.

SOCIAL AWARENESS

- Empathy, organizational awareness.
- Compassion for others.
- Service orientation.

RELATIONSHIP MANAGEMENT

- Inclusive, develops others, teamwork and collaboration.
- Inspirational leadership, change catalyst, influencer.
- Skilled conflict management.

PRACTICAL EQ

It is important to remember that demonstrating EQ boils down to little choices in actions and words. Practically speaking, this may just mean taking an extra moment before choosing your response the next time you feel challenged. Here are some examples.

EQ looks like:
- Dropping the drama.
- Moving out of complaint.
- Seeking benefits.
- Acknowledging your fallibility.
- Allowing yourself to feel the pain that you have caused others – notice the harm.
- Taking responsibility for your impact.

EQ sounds like:
- Genuine apologies: I am sorry I upset you.
- Open requests: Please help me understand why you see it that way?
- Appreciation: Thank you for everything you have done for me.
- Invitations to communicate more: Can we talk about it?
- Appropriate expression of emotion: I feel sad and angry that this is happening.

Increasing EQ feels:
- Challenging, scary and disorienting: at first, as you drop old patterns and behaviours.
- Strengthening, grounding, centring, stabilizing: as you learn new ways of relating.

EQ outcomes:
- Stability
- Appreciation
- Gratitude
- Forgiveness
- Compassion
- Open-heartedness
- Presence
- Inspiration
- Wisdom

Processing Difficult Emotions

If you are anything like me, you probably do not have many problems processing joy, laughter and love, but you may find anger, grief and fear a little trickier. But what if you could process these more challenging emotional states with the same openness that allows you to experience and process the warm and fuzzies?

Scientists have discovered that emotions arise, pass through the body and dissolve in ninety seconds. . . unless they are resisted, or you choose to rerun the circuit, firing a new round of thoughts that set the emotion off again. The lesson here is that the body is already adept at processing emotion, however the human psyche is not. As a result, both catastrophizing and rumination rear their heads again (see Lesson 6).

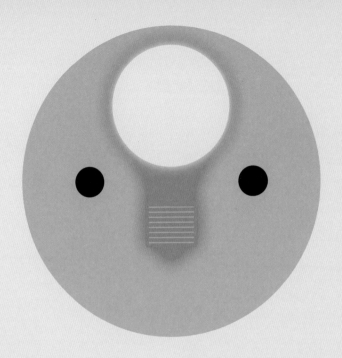

PRACTICE

01. ACCEPT
When you are feeling difficult emotions, start by simply accepting their presence. Remember the mindfulness maxim: *Acceptance precedes change.*

02. TURN TOWARDS
If your emotions seem manageable in their intensity, experiment by compassionately turning towards the feelings, allowing yourself to recognize and feel them. Bring them into focused awareness. Soften your resistance, knowing that you can turn away if it feels too much.

03. NAME IT
What is a good enough label for this emotion? It doesn't need to be perfect. Naming emotions allows you to take a little step back and gain perspective.

This is sadness. This is regret. This is confusion. . .

04. EXPRESS
Moving emotion into expression allows it to flow freely in and through you. If you are alone, vocalize it as a sound: a gasp, wail, laugh or sigh will do. Alternatively, take a blank sheet of paper, draw the outline of your body and use shading, lines, words and doodles to draw what you are feeling and where you experience it in the body.

05. LISTEN
Emotions are not always as meaningful as you might expect. Sometimes they are just passing through and occasionally they bring wisdom. Listen to check.

SELF-COMPASSION

What is self-compassion? Simply put, it is the skill of talking to and relating to yourself as you would a good friend.

At first glance, you might not think that self-compassion has much to do with leadership or excellence. In moments when you are actively leading others it might feel selfish or self-indulgent to think about self-compassion. And historically, self-compassion was associated with weakness, self-pity and a lack of motivation.

Research has since disproved all of these unfortunate preconceptions. In fact, practising self-compassion has been shown to build resilience and inner strength and help you to navigate the ups and downs of daily life. It has also been linked to enhanced wellbeing, motivation and, importantly, increased concern for others. Already you can see that it is starting to sound more like a leadership trait (linked as it is to increased emotional intelligence).

Remember too that leaders inspire others through their behaviours, actions and words. Those they lead feel a sense of common humanity with them and share largely similar goals. They are able to create this deeper impact through their own practice of self-compassion. Others sense the care with which they tend to themselves, and notice how this naturally extends to others.

Self-Compassion Exploration

If self-compassion describes the skill of relating to yourself internally in a kind and friendly way, why don't we all exhibit this trait? Research shows that many of us struggle with this.

The following writing exercise helps explore your current relationship with self, so give this one a try when you are feeling centred and clear. Self-compassion can be activating, so if you are going through a particularly tough time today, come back to this one later, or approach it with a friend or professional.

+ EXERCISE

Reflect on each question and write your answers in your notebook.

01. Imagine that a good friend comes to see you. They are really struggling with a personal problem.
- What sort of things would you say to them?
- What tone of voice would you use?
- What body language would you adopt (visualize yourself in the scenario)?

02. Now think of some behaviours you regularly struggle with. It could be at work, related to fitness, confidence or anything else.
- What sort of things do you say to yourself?
- What tone of voice do you use?
- How do you hold your body?

- What is the impact on the part of you that receives those words?
- If you are critical with yourself in this scenario, can you write some words of compassion to the part that receives the criticism?

03. Contemplate what might be the motivation for the critical voice (often referred to as the Inner Critic).

04. Are you able to write any words of compassion to the Inner Critic.

05. Close the exercise by writing some words of compassion to yourself.

WHY CULTIVATE SELF-COMPASSION?

You may have noticed that you share headspace with a powerful Inner Critic, who instead of being the champion of your striving and good intentions, will tell you every way in which you are deficient, unworthy, failing and undeserving. Its fearful voice is a manifestation of the threat response unhelpfully turned inwards. Here's how the fight, flight, freeze system translates into internal damaging behaviours.

THREAT RESPONSE TURNED INWARDS

Fight	Self-Criticism
	(Inner Critic)
Flight	Isolation
	(Self-Enforced)
Freeze	Rumination
	(Over-Identification)

Self-compassion reminds you that there is another way. Instead of falling into habitual patterns of self-criticism it is possible to tell yourself:

- I am doing my best.
- This is hard.
- I am dealing with a lot.
- I am struggling here and need some support.
- I have not done anything wrong.
- I am not in physical danger.
- I am loved.
- I am connected to other people and can choose to ask for help.
- I will get through this.
- I will be ok.

Remember that your track record for getting through tough days is 100 per cent so far. You will also get through this one.

PRACTICE

Soften, Soothe, Allow is a short practice of self-compassion created by leading researcher Kristin Neff PhD that you can do anytime you are having a tough day or feeling overwhelmed.

SOFTEN
Gently soften to your experience. Allow yourself to feel the pain, emotion or hurt. Breathe into it.

SOOTHE
Bring one or both hands to the part of you that is calling for attention, or simply hold your own hand. Imagine you were tending to a loved one.

ALLOW
If it feels ok, allow yourself to open and feel a little more of what is there. If it becomes too much you can always turn away. Remind yourself that you are human, and that you are compassionately attending and caring for the part of you that is hurting.

TWO PLANTS

In 2016 Ikea sponsored a creative experiment in a school in which two identical plants were given the same amount of water and sunlight, but one was played a recording of students saying mean things to it, and the other was played a recording of positive, affirming messages. Students passing by were also encouraged to taunt one and praise the other.

While the one that was being bullied struggled and grew weak, the one that received positive feedback visibly flourished. Whether the outcome was in fact scientifically sound wasn't the point; the students watched one plant suffer and wither, and the other grow beautifully, and learned a powerfully relatable visual lesson about the impact of bullying on their classmates.

Now, think back to the types of things you say to yourself when you are struggling. Which plant are you?

TOOLKIT

09

Stress is a necessary and natural component of life. Moving through your day with balance and ease requires a clear perspective on the different types of stressors you are facing, so you can allocate different amounts and qualities of attention and care to each. And when things get hairy, remember to ask yourself if you are in physical danger. If the answer is *no*, all you need is to STOP.

10

Embracing change does not come easy to most but is highly rewarding. There is no safety in the status quo, and all structures are impermanent and unstable. Learn to welcome the flow of shifting circumstances through your life, using proactive means of keeping clear and calm, which will help to develop the qualities of equanimity and serenity throughout the course of events.

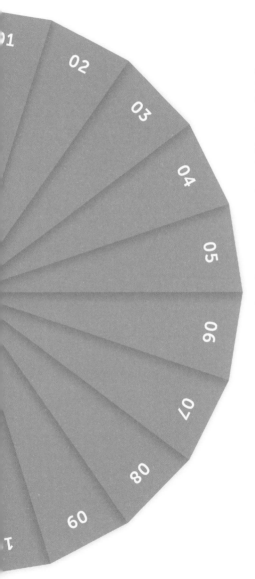

11

Emotional Intelligence is the most important leadership skill there is. Your EQ links with your ability to manage, inspire, motivate and influence. Developing this line of intelligence requires dedication to self-development and the willingness to explore difficult emotions in your mindfulness practice. In this way, you will grow in self-awareness, compassion and presence.

12

Self-compassion does not come naturally to many of us, yet it is powerful to explore what changes when we are able to approach ourselves in this different light. It turns out that developing self-compassion through short practices like *Soften, Soothe, Allow* (page 86) can also increase your wellbeing, motivation and concern for others. Win, win.

FURTHER LEARNING

READ

Omnibus: Emotional Intelligence and *Working with Emotional Intelligence* Daniel Goleman (Bloomsbury Publishing PLC, 2004)

Self-Compassion Kristin Neff PhD (Yellow Kite, 2011)

The Seven Spiritual Laws of Success: A Practical Guide to the Fulfillment of Your Dreams Dr Deepak Chopra (Bantam Press; reprint edition, 1996)

VISIT

The combined **Mindful Living Show/The Sleep Show** is an annual event, currently in London and Manchester, offering the latest developments in wellbeing, with a growing stream of content relevant to busy professionals: www.mindfullivingshow.com

LISTEN

'How To Make Stress Work For You' lectures by Kimberlee Bethany Bonura PhD (The Great Courses, 2017).

TRAIN

Kickstart your mindfulness practice and increase your stress resilience with a mindfulness course. There are many available online as well as in local studios. Find something close to you through www.bemindfulonline.com and www.eventslist.org

SELF-DEVELOPMENT

LESSONS

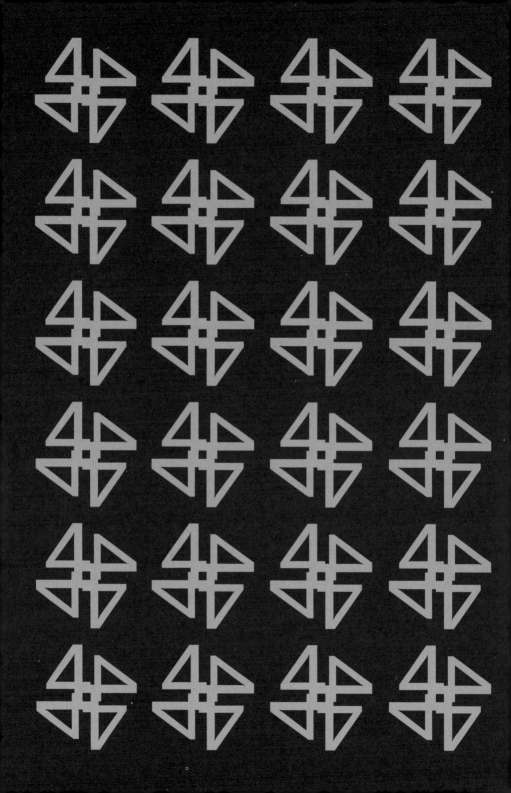

It is at the edges that interesting things happen. . . where one ecosystem meets another, where the old meets the new and where learning happens.

Anyone reading this book is already invested and committed to their own development. And as someone seeking knowledge and skills you are also very likely to have found out that your greatest teachings arrive when you least expect them, or when you are pushed out of your comfort zone into a space of risk and vulnerability. This dynamic yet scary learning zone is sandwiched between the edges of comfort and chaos.

It is worth remembering that it is at the edges that interesting things happen. Whether it be hedgerows at the side of a field, the leading edge of a grass roots political movement, or the edge of your assumptions, here is a place where one ecosystem meets another, where the old meets the new and where learning happens. Self-development therefore asks you to put yourself into some uncomfortable places: to volunteer for that big presentation, to take on a task that stretches your knowledge, to put yourself back in the classroom.

When it comes to lifelong learning, the Japanese principle of Kaizen is worthy of note. (*Kai* means change and *zen* means wisdom.) As a concept, Kaizen is often summarized as the teaching of continuous improvement. It has relevance not just to the journey of self-development, but to the efficiency and performance of processes, groups and businesses.

Kaizen asks you to consider the following: no matter how well something is going today, how can you improve it tomorrow? It keeps you searching for beneficial developments, micro and macro, and keeps the threat of attachment to the comfortable status quo at bay. When leading others, you can implement the principle by naming it as important to you, and then explaining how you would like your team to start working with it. As they do so, ensure that you regularly acknowledge those that go above and beyond, taking performance that is already good, to the next level. In this way, the principle can become embedded as a way of thinking and a way of working.

In the following lessons we look at how to incorporate this powerful principle into your self-development work through mindfulness, gratitude, happiness and heartfulness.

MINDFULNESS

Mindfulness is not new. Within every wisdom tradition you will find a version of a practice of silence, be it meditation, prayer, contemplation, retreat, yoga, devotional movement or other. There is a lesson here. Silence, or stillness, is a foundational need for human beings. Rather than being designed to continuously consume experience, our physiology is optimized to perform best when sufficient time and space is offered to not only sleep, but digest and integrate our experiences in moments of quiet alertness. It is therefore very good news that mindfulness has appeared on the world stage at this time, as a simple and secular practice of silence.

As a tool, mindfulness allows you to navigate your interior self (your thoughts, emotions and body sensations) with increased skill, enabling you to map these intimate spaces as you process the outer reality of life. It can help people deal effectively with stressful situations, cope with (or overcome) anxiety and depression, or simply bring a sense of calm and purpose to your life.

MORNING RITUAL
Think carefully where your mindfulness practice will fit in to your morning routine. The aim is to make it part of your habitual activities, so you do not even have to think about it. It just happens. For example, if you always shower, dress, eat breakfast, prep lunch and leave the house, get up five minutes earlier so you can meditate between

dressing and eating. And yes: five minutes is absolutely worthwhile, and 100 per cent better than no minutes. Similarly, do not feel that you need to practise every single day.

Make sure you have a few comforts around you, a favourite cushion, blanket, timer and notebook. (Leave your phone elsewhere – it is mindfulness kryptonite.) Set your timer for between five and ten minutes, and set an intention to be present with the practice until the timer rings. Close your eyes and follow this path, starting at the beginning each time you find yourself distracted:

Breath > Body > Emotion > Mind > Self

01. Breath
Follow the breath into the body, riding the inhalations and exhalations.

02. Body
Notice the rise and fall of the chest. Feel the sensation of clothing moving against skin, and the weight of the body pushing down into your seat.

03. Emotion
Label the obvious emotions that are present.

04. Mind
Notice there are thoughts, and spaces between the thoughts. Settle into the gaps.

05. Self
Enquire: what does it feel like to be me in this moment?

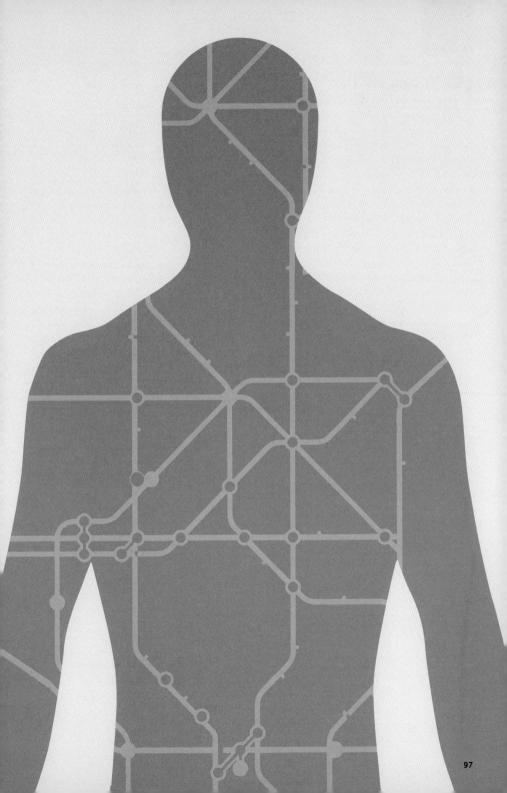

THROUGHOUT THE DAY

It is very easy to forget your morning mindfulness practice within a few hours of getting into your day. It is therefore helpful to integrate some gentle reminders into your schedule to bring you back to mindful awareness. Even taking a conscious breath now and then will help you do this. Eckhart Tolle, author of *The Power of Now*, teaches that: 'A single conscious breath is a meditation'.

So why not pick three mindfulness cues: one sound, one object and one person, and each time they show up in your day, take a conscious breath and remember who you are. As this becomes a habit, you may notice that you start to utilize this simple technique when you sense uncertainty or are feeling challenged.

Conscious Breath

You take a conscious breath by inhaling, knowing that you are inhaling, feeling the physical sensations of the breath moving into the body, and then exhaling, knowing that you are exhaling, feeling the physical sensations of the breath leaving the body.

CIRCUIT BREAKERS

Here are some of the common barriers to mindfulness, and how to find your way back to the meditation cushion:

My Mind is Too Busy

This is the number one reason for giving up. Yet if you have a busy mind, all it means is that you are human, and alive. An important focus for mindfulness practice is to gently teach the mind that it is safe to reside in thought-free awareness (silence). This is a big learning for your brain, as most minds are preoccupied with the job of keeping you out of danger and on task. It takes time for the mind to relax, slow, and offer up a little silence. Stick with it. You are on the right track.

I Don't Have Time to Practise

What most people actually mean when they give the time excuse is this: *I do not*

MINDFULNESS CUE	EXAMPLES
01. One Sound	Phone ringing/vibrating
	Doorbell
	Birdsong
02. One Object	Postbox
	Your reflection
	Brake lights
03. One Person	Your partner
	Your child
	A colleague

consider mindfulness important enough to add to my schedule. Which is fine, if that is true, but don't kid yourself that it is a time thing. Sure – you are busy. You have all of those commitments, responsibilities and activities. Yet you also manage to browse online shopping, keep up with social media and watch your favourite TV shows. So if you think mindfulness is important, it's time to get professional and invest those five minutes.

Guilt

It is easy to start associating mindfulness practice with the guilt you feel when you do not practise. This is very common and completely understandable. If you fall out of your meditation routine, remind yourself that you must first practise self-forgiveness and then mindfulness. Both are powerful.

That's Enough Presence and Peacefulness, Thank You

This sounds like an odd one, but when you have a mature mindfulness practice, this rather strange circuit breaker appears. You have become familiar with journeying to stillness and sorting through your interior world, yet there is an itch that pops you out of practice, perhaps accompanied by the thought – *I've done my peacefulness today, so let's get on with the to-do list.* This one is also worth breaking through. Patiently sit in the peace, watching the urges to leave come and go. Mindfulness students who continue to develop have evolved the capacity to open further within the expanse of silence.

GRATITUDE AND GENEROSITY

Gratitude is a wisdom practice, yet one that does not come naturally to human beings. While there are likely more things that are wonderful in your world than terrible, the internal Editor-in-Chief of your *Daily Thought Stream* prefers dramatic scare-stories over feel-good fables, and the DJ in your head plays *misery* at top volume, and *good-times-chill-out* on low. Don't worry, though – as you discovered in Lesson 6, it's not you, it's your brain.

Turning these natural neural propensities around is like developing a completely new content strategy for your inner broadcast channels: not easy. That said, it is absolutely worthwhile, given all of the ways that gratitude has been shown to change and strengthen the brain in astoundingly beautiful ways, not to mention improving your quality of life.

Gratitude does this by redirecting your attention towards things to be grateful for

GIFTS OF GRATITUDE

INCREASES	General wellbeing, alertness, generosity, compassio
STRENGTHENS	Social connection, immune system, capacity for joy
IMPROVES	Sleep, resilience, mental and physical health, (lower
REDUCES	Stress, depression, anxiety, addiction

and reminding you to experience them more deeply. The intention is to notice positive experiences and, as a result, your awareness becomes attuned to the little things that happen each day that are worth appreciating.

You might think that suddenly becoming a lot more grateful sounds rather contrived. After all, your appreciation settings have formed over many years, and may feel synonymous with your personality. So before considering the practices that follow, take a little inventory of all the things that you find it easy to appreciate already. This helps you remember that you are looking to increase something that is already there, not for something new. You already know what gratitude feels like, your only aim is to feel it more frequently, and more abundantly. This is the journey from negativity to positivity, and from complaint to appreciation.

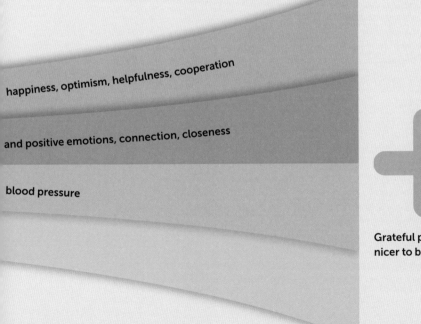

happiness, optimism, helpfulness, cooperation

and positive emotions, connection, closeness

blood pressure

Grateful people are nicer to be around

PRACTISING GRATITUDE

Becoming more grateful is not just experientially beneficial for you, but creates an energy of appreciation that moves from you as a leader into the wider network of those you impact directly and indirectly. The following practices allow you to put the science to work and investigate what occurs in your teams, relationships and at home as you increase your capacity for gratitude.

PRACTICE

The brain likes consistency and novelty. The most beneficial gratitude practices from a neural point of view are therefore those that happen regularly but focus on new or different things each time.

THREE THINGS FOR 21 DAYS

Every day, write down three things that you are grateful for. This might include workplace triumphs, memorable moments with friends or even appreciation for how well you handled a difficult scenario. While you will start to notice some things that show up consistently, try to list three specific and novel things each day, rather than repeats. This will make the practice more rewarding and effective. As a variation — why not end your next team meeting with a round of gratitude shares?

THANK YOU

Gratitude is a universal human attribute, honoured in all peoples, and cultures, worldwide. Make eye contact and say thank you regularly throughout the day. Each time you say it, feel the vibration of the words. Think of it as a mini-meditation.

WRITE A LETTER

Spending twenty minutes writing a thank you letter to someone who impacted your life or career in a positive way has been shown to positively impact your capacity to feel gratitude and generosity, even three months after the exercise. Give it a go. It is the written expression of appreciation that is powerful; you can choose later if you want to send the letter or not.

RANDOM ACTS OF KINDNESS

There is a natural connection between gratitude and generosity. The more you feel you have to appreciate in life, the more you feel willing and able to share. An expression of gratitude is society's method of reinforcing generosity as a social norm.

Practising random acts of kindness is both fun and good for you. With benefits ranging from increased cardiovascular health to slowing the ageing process, the spreading of joy is contagious.

Here are some suggestions to get you going:

- Browse a book store – buy something uplifting, write a little message to the new owner and leave it somewhere to be found by a passer-by.
- Buy a couple of extra mini-umbrellas and keep them in your car or bag. Next time you pass someone caught in the rain, offer one with a smile and walk away.
- Next time you're at the toll booth, pay for yourself and the car behind you.
- Make some snacks at home and take them to work for your colleagues.
- When you use a vending machine, leave some change in the machine for the next person.
- Make a family member breakfast in bed.

INHALE. FE
BREATH IN
BODY. EXH
LET GO.

EL THE
THE
ALE.

THE HAPPY LEADER

We're all at our best when happy, and most of us would like to experience more happiness. Yet contentment can be both elusive and complicated, which means for most it is very much a work in progress.

Maintaining an attitude of happiness long-term is a highly demanding practice as it requires the inner strength to seat the mind consistently in uplifted equanimity, irrespective of the rise and fall of circumstance. It also demands the courage to face all the barriers to happiness that you have accumulated, and faithfully tear them down. This is certainly deep work.

There are some misdirects at play here too: many modern cultures point to material and creature comforts, as well as influence and power, as the source of happiness. Yet as the newly rich and powerful soon learn, it is possible to have every wealth and luxury and still be utterly miserable. With happiness, there are no shortcuts.

Like gratitude, happiness derives from embracing the good – noticing and taking in the joy-giving things that are already present in your life. By doing this we can overcome the negativity bias of the brain, which tends to cling to worries and negative experiences and slide over positive ones.

PRACTICE

01. Follow your breath towards mindful presence.

02. As you notice the rise and fall of the chest, bring to mind something that happened in the last 24 hours that made you smile and brought a sense of happiness.

03. Allow the memory to become brighter and clearer. Recall the finer details.

04. Feel the happiness and warmth again. Perhaps the smile even returns to your lips.

05. Stay with the feeling as it grows and spreads through your body.

06. As you breathe, imagine the feeling of happiness and appreciation vibrating through the body. Stay with the experience for five more cycles of breath.

07. Bring the practice to a close in your own time.

HAPPINESS NOW

Your happiness is determined 50 per cent by genetics, 10 per cent by circumstances and 40 per cent by your mindset, which informs your thoughts, actions and behaviours.

Yet there is a natural human tendency to miscalculate the impact of future circumstances on your outlook. This is *when/then* thinking and it keeps happiness in the distance rather than here in the now. This way of thinking also means that your happiness is only accessible fleetingly when you become something, get something or achieve something.

When/then thinking sounds a bit like this:

When I am...........................then I will be happy.
When I have........................then I will be happy.
When I have achieved.......then I will be happy.

How does your brain normally fill in these blanks?

01. Write your sentences in your notebook.

02. Is there a way that you can rework your sentences to bring happiness within reach right now?

When I make partner, **then** I will be happy.

Becomes: **I am happy** working towards my ambition of becoming a partner at my firm.

If you spot *when/then* thinking creeping into your life, develop the habit of finding your happiness in the present moment. After all, the time is always now.

HAPPINESS AT WORK

Workplace relationships are both complicated and important. They can be a source of great comfort and happiness and/or the catalyst for significant suffering. Keeping perspective when navigating the inevitable office politics will help you hold on to contentment even in the tricky arena of work. Keep in mind the following:

You Are Marmite

Not everyone is going to like you, or be your best friend, so you will waste a lot of time and mental energy if you enter work with that goal. The fact that your vibe goes down well with some and not others says nothing about you, other than you are a human like the rest of us. Accepting that reality frees you up to be content simply being yourself around others.

Be Yourself

Everyone feels more comfortable around authenticity coupled with an appropriate dash of vulnerability. As you invest time getting to know the people you work with, being yourself means opening up about aspects of your life at home, your hopes and dreams, your worries and failings. This takes courage and trust, so go at your own pace.

Keep Things Clear

If someone is bothering you at work, or a relationship is turning sour, it is highly likely that you will start having negative thoughts, which may turn into a list of complaints. This happens because the brain starts to see the relationship as a potential threat to your survival, which is why the possibility of being thought poorly of, or ostracized, activates such a powerful stress response.

Keep your behaviour and communication in check by:

01. **Noticing that you are activated by their behaviour and your thoughts are becoming negative – this is your early warning system to check yourself.**
02. **Asking yourself: What else could this mean? Do I sometimes do that? Remember that we rarely know the full picture and our guesses and assumptions are not facts.**
03. **Instead of taking the situation personally, breathe, re-engage your best self and approach the situation with mindful compassion.**

Networking with Radical Honesty

When it comes to networking with people you are meeting for the first time, my favourite play is radical honesty. People are so bored by the general back and forth of *What do you do and where do you work*, that going in with something unexpectedly honest like *I'm absolutely starving* goes so much further towards breaking the ice and inspiring presence. It is more fun, too!

THE SCIENCE OF HEART

The most interesting thing about your heart is not that it beats 100,000 times a day (that's 2.5 billion times per average lifetime), or that it is the first organ to form in the human body, but that it processes information through its own intrinsic nervous system, so sophisticated that it has become known as the *Heart Brain*. That's right, your heart has a mind of its own.

The heart is also the most powerful electro-magnetic organ in the body and sends the very first electrical signal to the brain of the human foetus, directing its form and function. As it communicates with the brain, you may be surprised to know that it delivers more information than it receives, the brain interpreting the signals of the heart to decide how to feel and respond.

The rhythm of the heartbeat transmits the level of coherence of your internal emotional state, and this is linked with your rate of respiration and the rhythm of your blood pressure. While you emit a stable and coherent pattern when you experience positive emotions such as love and appreciation, anger and frustration produce incoherent patterns. These frequencies are felt by you first, but then feed into the connecting electromagnetic field, impacting those around you. Disturbances in this field (incoherent patterns) can be perceived as tension, for example in a room where an argument has just occurred.

As a leader, you are often responsible for setting the energy in a meeting or at an event. In order to access clarity, intuition and wise decision-making in yourself and others, heart coherence is optimal. Breathing exercises, happiness and mindfulness practices will help you increase your experience of coherence.

As leadership styles evolve from *Command and Control* to more *Conscious* models, there opens a space for heart coherence and emotional intelligence to inform intellectual analysis. Take a look at the comparison table and consider which model of leadership resonates most with you.

COMMAND AND CONTROL	CONSCIOUS LEADERSHIP
IQ	EQ+IQ
Authority-Based	Values-Based
Limited Awareness	Global Awareness
Manipulation	Influence and Right Action
Clinical	Empathic and Compassionate
Competitive	Cooperative and Collaborative
Unaware of Limitations	Self-Aware

HEART OF THE LEADER

Developing heart coherence allows you to access the deeper potentials of the Conscious Leadership paradigm. By actively taking care of your interiority, your behaviours become consistent and it becomes easier to develop trust and respect within your team. Your colleagues begin to notice that you are speaking and acting from a space of common humanity and this translates to increased influence, which motivates, engages and inspires.

While you may fear that this paradigm does not offer the power available to you within the *Command and Control* model, there is a potent catalyzing impact here, sometimes described as soft power.

Beyond this, the outcomes that arise within this model have the greatest potential to be imbued with presence, right action, harmony, alignment and wisdom. The overall frequency here is that of professional excellence. This then is the Heart of The Leader, inspired by the writings of Heartfulness expert, Ravi Venkatesan.

PRACTICE

This heart-focused practice allows you to experience the frequency of coherence.

01. Take a deep, calming breath and allow your breathing to fall into a steady and comfortable rhythm.
02. Place one or both palms over the centre of your chest.
03. Imagine someone you love in front of you. Feel the flow of energy between you. Sense the rhythm and frequency of this heartful vibration.
04. Inhale, visualizing your breath moving towards and into your heart.
05. Exhale, feeling the electro-magnetic energy of the heart radiating outwards.
06. As you continue breathing, explore the felt sensations in and around the heart, noticing sensations, images and emotions.
07. End with a sense of gratitude and appreciation for those you love.

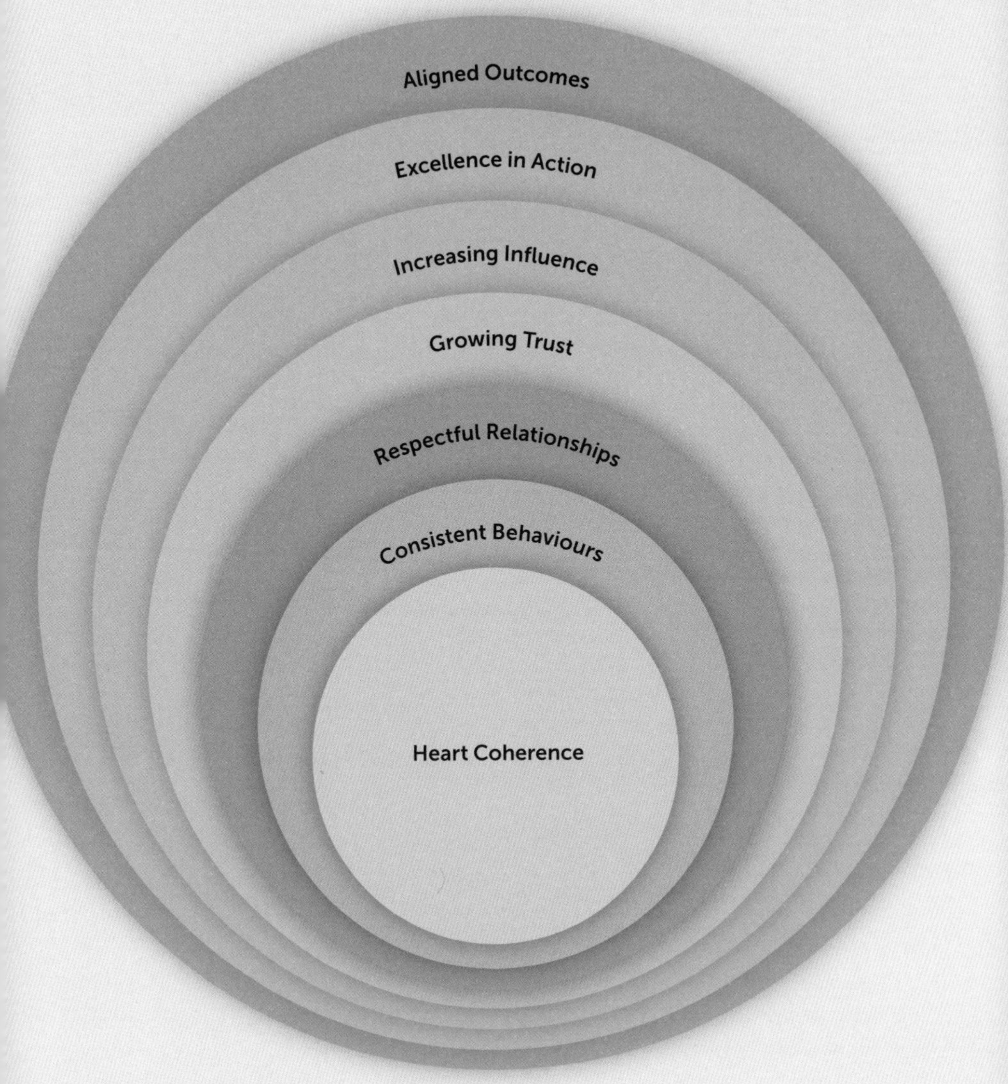

Aligned Outcomes

Excellence in Action

Increasing Influence

Growing Trust

Respectful Relationships

Consistent Behaviours

Heart Coherence

TOOLKIT

13

Navigating your interior world of thoughts, emotions and sensations is complicated work. Mindfulness is the map. Through simple practices we learn how to explore what is already there, just below the surface. Building mindfulness into your morning routine, as well as coming back to presence briefly (and frequently) during the day, can help you shift towards your centre, and meet challenges with a clear head.

14

The practice of gratitude enables us to navigate from fearfulness to resilience. Whatever occurs within the tapestry of life, there are always things to be grateful for. And one of the simplest ways of bringing more gratitude into your life is by saying thank you more frequently and more completely. What are you grateful for today?

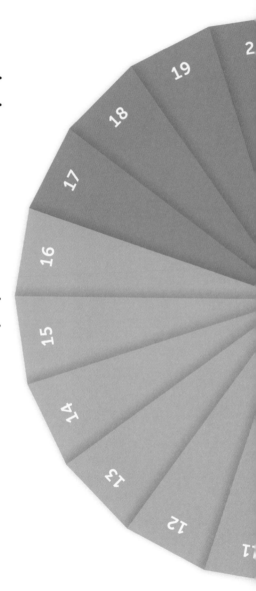

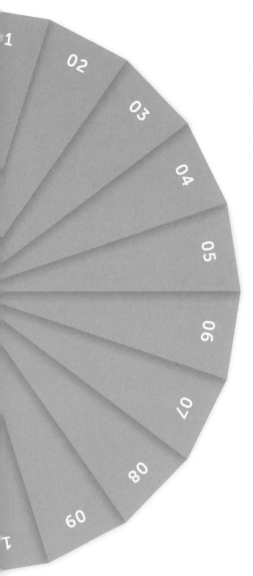

15

Happiness is usually not that far away.
Sometimes all it needs is a shift in attention
to remember some of the beautiful moments
that may have passed you by today.
Happiness is definitely not something to be
delayed, so make sure you are not placing
arbitrary barriers between your happiness
and your present moment experience. All of
your happiest moments occurred squarely in
the *now*.

16

The heart allows us to stay connected, and
to find compassion for ourselves and those
around us. It also allows us to lead with
increased focus on working cooperatively,
collaboratively and consciously. By
practising with the heart, you can deepen
your connection to your common humanity
and become an even more influential and
inspiring leader.

FURTHER LEARNING

READ

100 Mindfulness Meditations, The Ultimate Collection of Inspiring Daily Practices
Neil Seligman (Conscious House, 2016)

Dare to Lead: Brave Work. Tough Conversations. Whole Hearts
Brené Brown (Vermilion, 2018)

Hardwiring Happiness: How to reshape your brain and your life
Rick Hanson (Rider, 2014)

Joy on Demand: The Art of Discovering the Happiness Within
Chade-Meng Tan (HarperOne, 2016)

DOWNLOAD

The Chill App sends you mindful awareness reminders throughout the day, at intervals of your choice.

The Buddhify App is a beautiful meditation app with a distinctive user interface and relevant meditations for daily life.

RESEARCH

The Heartmath Institute has been researching the science of the heart and developing tools to help people reduce stress while experiencing more peace, satisfaction and enjoyment since 1991. www.heartmath.org

Heartfulness Magazine is online at www. heartfulnessmagazine.com – in particular I recommend a series of articles called 'The Heartful Leader' by Ravi Venkatesan.

PLAY

Happify offers tools and programs to help you take control of your feelings and thoughts. www.happify.com

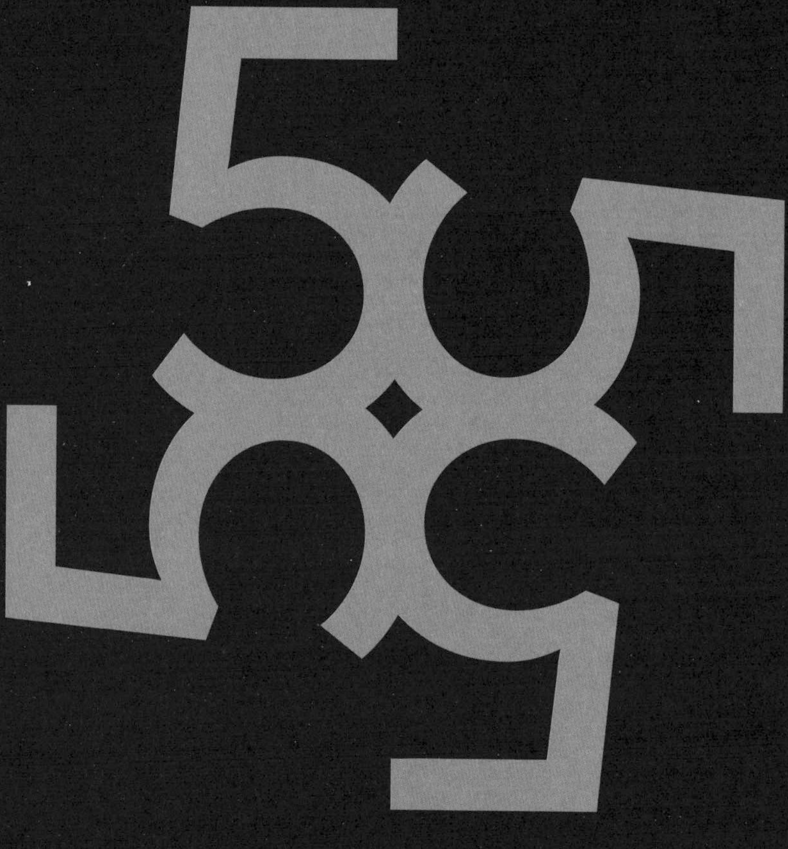

SELF-REALIZATION

LESSONS

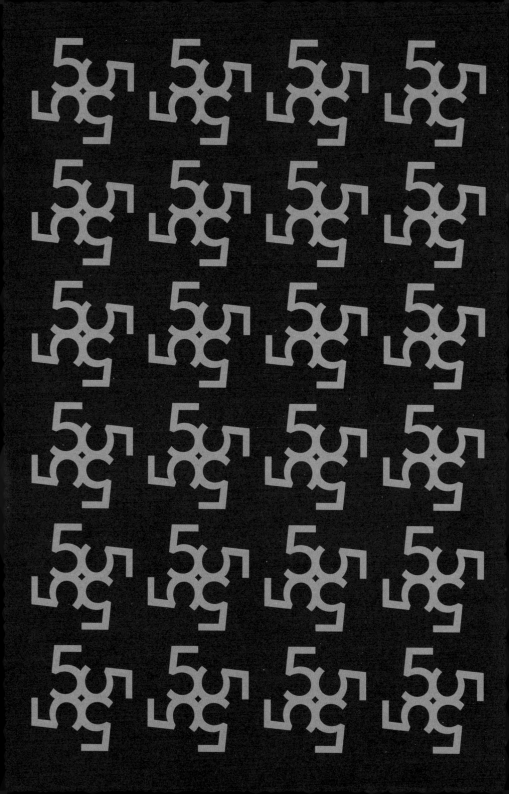

Rather than being something to plan or search for, moments of self-realization often find you when you least expect them.

You have been on the path of self-realization ever since you first looked in the mirror as an infant and wondered who the moving, smiling, curious creature was staring back at you. One day a deeply important truth landed within you, and you knew the face in the mirror was your own.

In that moment, you learned that you had identity, power and autonomy. Later, you discovered your desires, ambitions, likes, dislikes, hopes and dreams. For the human being is a remarkable creation, which, like peeling away an onion, reveals itself layer by layer.

Rather than being something to plan or search for, moments of self-realization often find you when you least expect them. As Enneagram – a personality-typing tool utilized in modern psychology

– luminary Russ Hudson says, 'You never know when the Universe is going to wink at you!' So rather than toiling towards self-realization, the patient student of life and leadership satisfies themselves by setting out to ace the ordinary moments of the day-to-day, bringing to each their best self, a learning mind and a growing capacity to both succeed and fail well. In doing so, the extraordinary Eureka moments, the 'Ah-ha's and the revelations take care of themselves.

It is common to both crave and fear self-realization as it requires us to experience and then take responsibility for our interconnectedness and shared reality. In the lessons that follow, we build skills that take us towards that goal as we consider leadership capacities, excellence, vulnerability, creativity and alignment.

LEADERSHIP CAPACITIES

How many times have you been engaged in an important conversation with a friend or colleague when you sensed that instead of really listening, they were actually formulating their next soundbite (reloading)? Even before you've finished your point, they are chiming in with their thoughts, often having failed to acknowledge or understand the point you were actually making. Perhaps sometimes you even notice yourself doing this too?

This common experience stems from one of the biggest challenges of our time: listening effectively. Without high-quality listening, we miss vital data and the opportunity to see the full picture, limiting our effectiveness overall.

How to Listen With Awareness

Conscious listening means listening with awareness. It is characterized by alert presence and openness. It creates a space that is not filled with content (your thoughts, concerns and predictions) but with the energies of welcoming, non-judgement and genuine curiosity. Its impact is to allow the other person the safety to be seen, heard, acknowledged and understood. When you are offered this quality of listening, it feels both freeing and empowering. Sadly, you may also notice how rare it is to be treated in this way.

If you choose to experiment with conscious listening you may find it helpful to reflect on the following questions to chart your progress. If conscious listening is new to you, it may take a little time to feel at ease with it, but trust the process and see what happens.

01. **How does listening with awareness affect the quality of information that you receive?**
02. **What impact does this shift in listening have on the sense of connection you feel with others?**
03. **What do you notice about your capacity to respond when you have listened consciously?**

HOW TO CREATE A CONSCIOUS BUSINESS

As leadership becomes more conscious, so businesses begin to reflect conscious values. Creating a conscious business requires bringing awareness to the characteristics below and welcoming some of the difficult conversations that arise when these philosophies meet the marketplace.

DO NO HARM

As a baseline, conscious businesses operate with an explicit intention to move towards systems, processes, products and services that do no harm to humans and the environment.

THE TRIPLE BOTTOM LINE

Instead of harnessing the single driver of profit, conscious businesses measure success by providing positive value to the three Ps:

01. PEOPLE

The business aims to contribute beneficially to the lives of its staff as well as all stakeholders, from manufacturers to suppliers, local communities and humanity overall. In practice this might include championing wellbeing in the workplace, improving employee benefits, using fair trade materials, or assisting communities involved in the supply chain and manufacturing.

02. PLANET

The conscious business model seeks to support responsible stewardship of the Earth, minimizing any negative impact on the environment and investing in replenishment where possible. Initiatives range from recycling, to using renewable energy, to purchasing from suppliers that share this value, to urging stakeholders to move towards conscious practices.

03. PROFIT

Conscious businesses seek to balance the concerns of profit against the values of people and planet and honour all three when it comes to decision-making.

HONEST FEEDBACK

The purpose of feedback is to offer a valuable acknowledgement, reflection or opinion, so the person who receives it may be inspired to take a new action or choose a different behaviour. At the same time, it is an opportunity to welcome and listen for new information, of which you are currently unaware. Keep your focus on both delivering your feedback with clarity and compassion and eliciting further information, which will help you enter the discussion with a clear purpose and an open mind.

Let's look at this in practice.

Be Honest

Take full responsibility for your point by making it clear you are expressing your views. Do not hide behind the opinions of people not present.

Be Consistent

Hold everyone to the same standard, including yourself. Ask yourself: if I was managing myself, what constructive feedback would I give me?

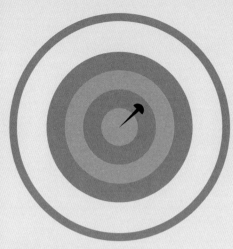

Be Specific
Lead with the facts and ask if they are agreed. Listen. Next come your observations, your opinions and your requests.

Ask For Their View
Have I missed any relevant information? What is your view on the situation? Listen with awareness.

Be Compassionate
An intention of compassion, connection and common humanity will help your feedback conversation remain positive, and allow messages to be received in the spirit that they are intended.

Get Agreement
Agree on what is going to change, often on both sides. If no agreement emerges, agree on what the barriers to agreement are and what the next practical step will be.

EXCELLENCE

Ever missed a deadline, or sent your work late because you were continually perfecting the layout and wording over and over again, despite it being ready? That behaviour stems from a perfectionist mindset and is something that affects countless professionals and aspiring leaders.

Whether it is unrealistic expectations of the quantity and/or quality of your output, the human desire for excellence and status (by being seen to do well) can easily become a disproportionate preoccupation. Perfectionism is also something that can easily spill over from work tasks into home life and family interactions.

Beyond feeling more relaxed and capable, there is good reason to soften your approach to excellence, as the science surrounding perfectionism is salutary. As a trait, perfectionism can negatively impact performance, contribute to unhappiness and lead to anxiety or depression. Optimalism, on the other hand, is a conscious and compassionate version of perfectionism. You can still reach peak performance through optimalism, and you (and the people around you) will have a better experience getting there. The following chart, contrasting the perfectionist and the optimalist, is inspired by the work of Professor Tal Ben-Shahar.

PRACTICE

When in the grip of perfectionism, this practice will allow you to calm, gain perspective, and let go of the need for absolute control.

01. Drop into mindful awareness by feeling the weight of the body pushing down into your seat. Give the muscles that you are most aware of permission to release and let go.
02. Next, bring your attention to the eyes. Can you feel their weight, shape and movements. Offer the eyes an invitation to let go. Observe what happens. Breathe. Let go.
03. Allow your awareness to move to the back of the neck and shoulders. Offer the overlapping interweaving muscles an invitation to let go. Breathe.
04. Bring your attention to the mind. Allow the warmth of your awareness to soften your perception of mind. Is the mind holding on tightly or trying to retain control of things outside your influence? Invite the mind to loosen its grip on these areas of challenge. Let go for a moment. Soften. Observe.
05. Breathe calmly until the practice feels complete.

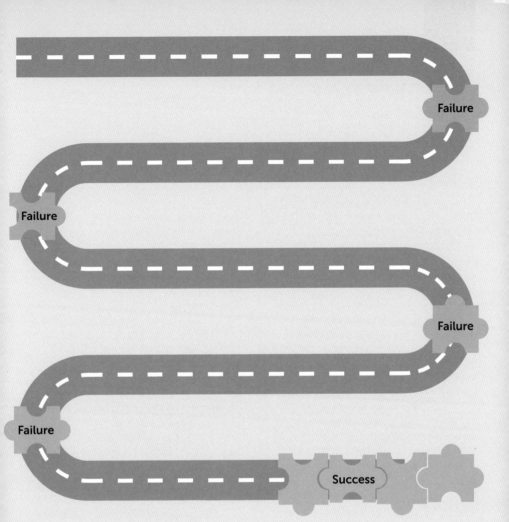

THE PERFECTIONIST	THE OPTIMALIST
Linear route to success	Non-linear route to success
Failure as fatal	Failure as feedback
Outcomes-focused	Outcomes- and journey-focused
Defensive, critical, harsh, inflexible	Welcoming, offers praise, dynamic
Rarely satisfied with achievement	Compassionate and forgiving
Unable to accept mistakes	Enjoys own and others' accomplishments
Tense attitude – tight grip	Realistic in managing mistakes
	Attentive and conscious attitude

THE VULNERABLE LEADER

There is no excellence without vulnerability, as anyone who has put themselves forward as a leader knows. Fallibility is built into the human being as standard and mistakes are part of the way we evolve and systems grow. In a fast-moving world, many roles require you to advise on (or predict) outcomes for uncertain futures. This task comes laden with risk and increases the likelihood of error and failure. It is therefore highly likely that in every ambitious life, circumstances will require you to accept, welcome and even learn to celebrate your vulnerabilities.

In accepting vulnerability you are acknowledging the difficult truth that your vision, values, intentions, hopes and dreams must all be translated from the formless realm of ideation, through the imperfect vessel of your human mind and body, into words, deeds and actions that fly or fall in a complex world. This is where the rubber meets the road, and theory comes face to face with reality.

It is here that, despite best efforts, all will sometimes fall short. These failings tend to drop individuals into one of the many perennial tales of human woe:

Do any of these sound familiar?
Does your personality have a favourite?

What you do next is a test of self-leadership. While these negative stories can be alluring and consuming, they are never true. Stay present, look around, ask for help. Ask yourself what it would feel like to be courageous, self-compassionate and to seek connection?

Human error, failures and suffering are built into the human experience for a reason. They inspire growth, course-correct and allow you to discover who you are becoming. Leadership is not about who can don the shiniest armour, it is about who can own their vulnerability, fragility and imperfection, and in so doing model authentic strength and bravery. Acknowledging vulnerability does not make you weak, it shows that you are relatable, humble, and inspires those around you to do the same. It gives others permission to occupy their own tender places, to share their scars and reveal their pain. These truths can be freeing, healing and transforming.

01. I am alone.
02. There is something wrong with me.
03. I am not enough.
04. I am unworthy of love.
05. Everything is futile.

✛ EXERCISE

As an exercise in courage, connection and self-compassion, here is a leadership development exercise that will give you an opportunity to experience your vulnerability, feel acknowledged and deepen relationships by gaining feedback from people you trust.

Reach out to four people from different areas of your life whose opinions you respect and value, and ask them to provide short answers to the following questions:

01. **What three words best describe me?**
02. **What do you value most about me?**
03. **What piece of advice or wisdom would you offer me, to help me grow?**
04. **What is the most important aspect of our connection for you?**

When the responses are in, reflect on the answers and make some notes on what you have learned. What are your top three takeaways?

LISTENING AWARENESS LEADER'S TOOL.

WITH

IS IS A

GREATEST

CREATIVITY AS STANDARD

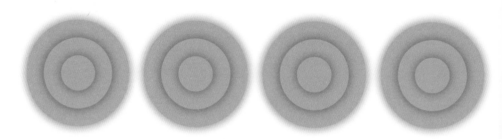

Contrary to popular belief, creativity is not the preserve of a small number of exceptional artists and illumined souls, it comes fitted as standard in every human body. So, if you left your creativity on a peg at school, I would like to invite you to retake ownership of it and to remember how to utilize this incredible resource. For creativity is the emergent state of all things, the field from which the new arises and a fertile place to seek inspiration. The Leonardo Da Vincis and Lady Gagas of this world are not more creative than you are, but they are fully immersed within the creative field and accomplished when it comes to harvesting those ideas. Creativity, then, is not a gift but a choice, and a skill that can be nurtured.

Creativity and mindfulness are related, too. They both arise from the same space of awareness. This is the realm of consciousness, characterized by the infinite or eternal, sometimes referred to in meditation as the *unending night sky*. It is within this space that silence resides along with the creative spark. And don't forget that idea-generation and problem-solving are creative skills, too.

Creative Leadership
In today's technologically accelerating world, creativity and the leadership of nimble, future-focused businesses is of high value. In fact, according to a global IBM survey of 1,500 Chief Executives, creativity is the number one most desirable leadership trait.

Creative leaders – whether running a family of three or a multinational – are insightful and imaginative. They know how to nurture their own creativity and that of their teams. By showing self-awareness, vulnerability and humility, creative leaders are able to generate a spirit of positivity that enables others to take risks from which creative solutions emerge. This leads to both increased productivity and innovation. Creative leaders are also passionate and

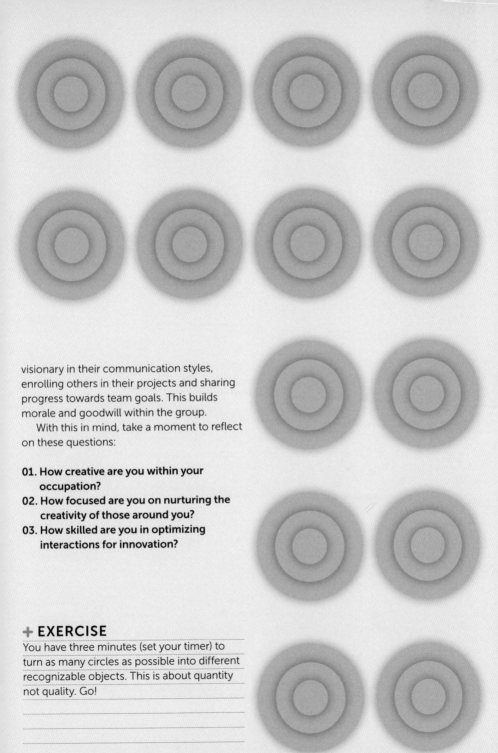

visionary in their communication styles, enrolling others in their projects and sharing progress towards team goals. This builds morale and goodwill within the group.

With this in mind, take a moment to reflect on these questions:

01. **How creative are you within your occupation?**
02. **How focused are you on nurturing the creativity of those around you?**
03. **How skilled are you in optimizing interactions for innovation?**

✛ EXERCISE

You have three minutes (set your timer) to turn as many circles as possible into different recognizable objects. This is about quantity not quality. Go!

CULTIVATING CREATIVITY

If you are wondering how to increase your creativity, or that of a team, know that there are some very practical research-backed activities that can do just that. Some of the suggestions in the following section are solo practices to experiment with yourself, while others are designed to support and re-energize the creative process within groups.

Daydream

With the advent of the smartphone and the evaporation of boredom, daydreaming happens less frequently, which is not good news for creativity. The human brain has two modes of attention. The task-positive network takes charge when actively focusing on an activity, while the task-negative network takes over for daydreaming. Eureka moments spark more frequently during task-negative time, so if you are stuck on a particular problem, take a break from scrolling screens, look out the window and let the mind wander.

Sleep On It

In a 1993 dream study by D. Barrett, 76 college students aged 19 to 24 were invited to sleep on their problems by focusing on a particular issue before drifting off. Approximately half the group had dreams that addressed their chosen problem, and over a quarter considered they had been offered solutions in their dreams! It was noted that when solutions arose overnight, the dreamt outcome also provided considerable personal satisfaction.

Create Too Much

The online positive news site Upworthy encourages its writers to create twenty-five different headlines for each article before choosing the best one. It just shows, you may already have something that is good, but the best may be yet to come.

Creative Meetings

As a starter, all meetings should aim to provide valuable take-aways for each attendee, whether it be through acknowledgement, relationship building, information exchange, clarification of goals/priorities or a chance to reflect on how to improve. But why not go beyond that and get creative, road-testing a new meeting format or developing your own.

Mindful Meeting

Instead of starting with the usual small talk, start with sixty seconds of silence. Frame it by saying something like: *'We are going to try something new today. This timer will go off in sixty seconds. Between now and then the invitation is to be silent and focus on your intention for the meeting'.*

Brainstorming Doodle

When leading a creative brainstorm, bring paper and colouring pens. Encourage attendees to doodle (on topic) as you go.

Goalfest

This weekly meeting format sees the whole team input personal weekly goals simultaneously into a shared spreadsheet to promote visibility, accountability and awareness of who is working on what.

Wins Meetings

A regular meeting to celebrate the wins, large and small, of your team. Participants can reflect on something they achieved personally, or commend another team member for their contribution. This goes a long way to inspiring a happy and productive culture.

Masterminds

This meeting format is for two people who are going to check in with each other regularly for support. For a one-hour meeting:

01. Take 10 minutes each to share updates and recent achievements.
02. Take 20 minutes each to talk through current challenges.

Instead of aiming to solve each other's problems by offering solutions and advice, the aim is to listen empathically and ask questions to help the other person solve their own issues.

ALIGNMENT

ALIGNMENT IS THE NEW SUCCESS

In the first line of this book I suggested that Conscious Leadership is the journey out of fear. It is also the journey into alignment.

Alignment means harmonizing who you are (primary) with what you do (secondary). After all, you are a *human being* not a *human doing*. Pursuing alignment in preference to success means that each time you reach a fork in the road, large or small, you ask yourself which path takes you closer into alignment with who you really are. You will know you are moving into alignment because it brings with it happiness and connects you with a sense of aliveness.

The most rewarding thing about trading the pursuit of success for alignment is that it takes you beyond the comparative state of mind. While there will always be others with more (and less) money, fame or power than you, alignment offers something richer: purposefulness and peacefulness.

Alignment is a little quieter than success, and once you have it, you don't need others to tell you well done. You will feel on track, centred in your integrity and respecting yourself wholeheartedly. Alignment also has a relationship with the energy of abundance. It is almost as if the universe hears you singing your own unique song with such gusto, that it starts to sing with you.

Conscious Leaders look to find alignment in themselves as well as nurturing it in the people around them. This might be through the management of team members, in seeking harmonic solutions for clients or inspiring their children.

But if the prospect of alignment seems far out of reach today, you might start gently by sitting with the following question for a few minutes: *What does life seek to do through me?* When you are done, make a note of any sensations, images, feelings or thoughts that came to you.

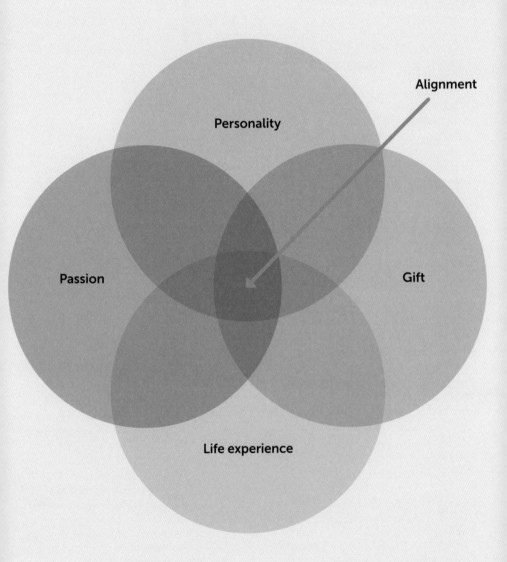

THE MOST IMPORTANT THING

As the saying goes, the most important thing is to remember the most important thing. Sounds so obvious, but there is a process here. You need:

01. **To know what the most important thing is.**
02. **To navigate the clamour of modern life, keeping that knowledge close.**
03. **Practices, such as those in this book, that bring you back to the most important thing (for when you forget).**

So, what is the most important thing to you in this moment?

What about in your life?

Remember you have done this work already, so check in with your vision and values. Has anything changed since you worked on those in previous lessons? How well have they stood up to the test of reality? How easily have you been able to keep them in mind when challenges rolled in? Take a moment to review them, and consider if there are any changes or adaptations you would like to make?

Next, with those reflections in mind, ask yourself: *What is my purpose?*

Write it down in a word, phrase or sentence. Say it out loud and see how it feels.

My purpose is: ....

Do not worry if it doesn't feel quite ready or complete. This exercise will always remain a work in progress, and your purpose may change and evolve as you grow.

PRACTICE

Having reached the end of your journey through Conscious Leadership, here is a final practice to allow you to reflect on the following three questions:

What are you ready to let go of?
What are you ready to open to?
What are you grateful for?

Imagine you are standing on a beautiful wooden bridge looking down at a freshwater stream as it flows from the hills around you over smooth grey rocks towards the waiting ocean.

You turn to face downstream and feel the energy of the water travelling beneath and away from you. You close your eyes and offer one thing you are ready to let go of, imagining it being carried away by the stream and transformed in the sea.

Next, you turn to face the fresh energy of the stream travelling towards you. As you feel its power, consider one thing you are ready to open to in your life. As it becomes clear, visualize it being carried to you by the approaching stream and receive it with open arms.

Finally, place your hands on your heart and feel the warmth of gratitude there.

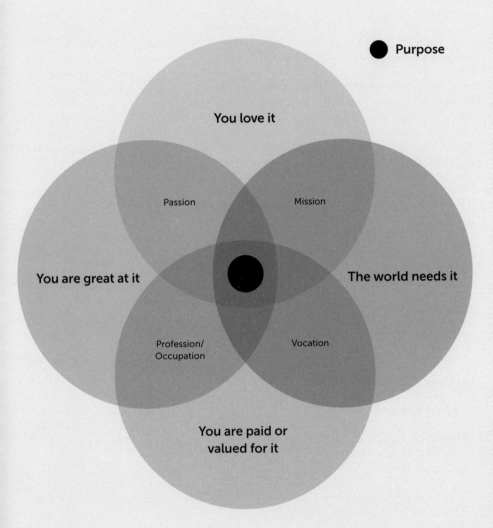

TOOLKIT

17

In order to lead well you must be able to listen spaciously and develop an appetite for honest feedback moving in both directions. These often overlooked skills are powerful and can set you apart from the competition.

18

The difference between perfectionism and optimalism is profound. While both champion high-performance and excellent outcomes, optimalism is also compassionate, realistic and human. Accepting our humanity by sharing vulnerabilities allows us to open, expand and connect with those around us.

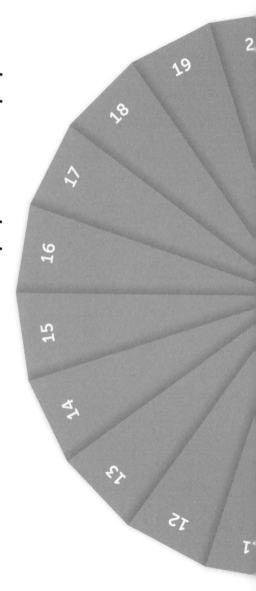

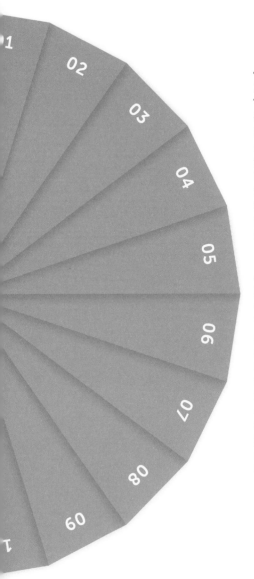

19

Creativity comes as standard in every human body. Sure, it needs acknowledging, nurturing and expressing, but it is absolutely there and available to you right now. Whether you are looking to lead with innovation and insight, or wondering how to cultivate creativity in others, there are practical tools to draw on to turn your intentions into actions.

20

The path of Conscious Leadership is the path towards alignment. With increased awareness you can come to better understand your calling, your gifts and your uniqueness. This valuable bounty of self-knowledge can then translate into powerful choices that lead you closer and closer to alignment – a space where purpose and joy meet your passion and vocation. Take a moment to reflect, and notice how far you have come.

FURTHER LEARNING

READ

Focus: The Hidden Driver of Excellence
Daniel Goleman (Bloomsbury Paperbacks, 2014)

Drawdown: The Most Comprehensive Plan Ever Proposed to Reverse Global Warming
Paul Hawken (Penguin, 2018)

The Pursuit of Perfect
Tal Ben-Shahar (McGraw Hill, 2009)

The Mind of the Leader: How to Lead Yourself, Your People, and Your Organization for Extraordinary Results
Rasumus Hougard and Jacqueline Carter (Harvard Business Review Press, 2018)

Care of the Soul: An inspirational programme to add depth and meaning to your everyday life
Thomas Moore (Piatkus, 2012)

TRY

Upworthy is on a mission to change what the world pays attention to by telling stories about important issues that connect us and sometimes even change the world. www.upworthy.com

Positive News is a constructive journalism magazine publishing independent journalism and aiming to create a more inspiring news medium. www.positive.news

LISTEN

'The Psychology of Performance, How to Be Your Best in Life' lectures by Eddie O'Connor PhD (The Great Courses, 2017)

VISIT

For inspiration from world experts on business, consciousness, mindfulness and technology, the **Wisdom 2.0 Conferences** are an incredibly rich resource of learning and community. The main conference assembles annually in San Francisco, attracting thousands of delegates from around the world. www.wisdom2summit.com

EPILOGUE

As the book comes to a close, I want to both thank and congratulate you for diving in and doing the work. I hope you have found the journey useful and rewarding.

As with all things, in every ending, there is also a beginning, and as the last page turns, a glorious moment awash with potential and choice opens to you. Perhaps use the opportunity to take stock of all of your accomplishments, notice your many gifts, appreciate your continued diligence, and with gratitude for staying the course, acknowledge yourself as the Conscious Leader that you are.

Standing at this opening may also offer a moment to reflect on the questions and learnings you are taking forward from here. If there are specific new actions that you will take, now is a good time to make some notes and harness your inspiration. And if you wish to continue the work of this book, ask yourself the following question and set yourself up for a year of gentle follow-up:

What insight, idea or question seems important right now that you hope to remember in a week, a month, a year?

Then create three reminders (at those intervals, or on dates of your choice) with a prompt to reflect on a certain topic, sit with a question or remember an important personal insight.

You have probably noticed that the book has been designed to leave you with more questions than answers, so if you are feeling like a work in progress, and that many lessons lie ahead, you are doing it just right. Remember that wisdom is always preceded by confusion, and you are therefore exactly where you need to be.

Finally, might I add that our world is in desperate need of Conscious Leaders courageously committed to self-knowledge,

Our world is in desperate need of Conscious Leaders. . . And by that, I mean Conscious Leaders like you.

skilled in self-maintenance, capable of self-management, working on self-development and on the path of self-realization. And by that, I mean Conscious Leaders like you.

If you are hesitating, please feel encouraged; know that there is never a moment when you will feel completely ready (even when you are doing it), but there will be a moment that powerfully invites you to stand up and be counted, and to step bravely into your destiny. My wish for you is that in that moment, the work that we have done together helps you to feel a little safer, more capable, more in touch with your magnificence, more connected to your internal resources and ultimately more acknowledged as the brilliant human being that you are.

In closing, I invite you to continue on this journey, becoming everything that you were born to be.

BIBLIOGRAPHY

CHAPTER 1

Kostadin Kushlev & Elizabeth W Dunn, 'Checking email less frequently reduces stress', *Computers in Human Behavior*, 43, pp220–228 (2015)

Frances Booth, **The Distraction Trap** (Pearson, 2013)

Roman Krznaric and The School of Life, **How to Find Fulfilling Work (The School of Life)** (Macmillan, 2012)

Joseph Jaworski and Peter M Senge, **Synchronicity: The Inner Path of Leadership** (Berrett-Koehler, 2011)

CHAPTER 2

Elemental Alchemy blog. Beautiful writings on ayurvedic wisdom for modern healthy living:
www.elemental-alchemy.com/blog/

James Joyce, **Dubliners** (Penguin Modern Classics, 2000)

Anna Halprin, **Return to Health: with Dance, Movement and Imagery** (LifeRhythm, U.S, 2002)

CHAPTER 3

Kelly McGonigal, **The Upside of Stress: Why stress is good for you (and how to get good at it)** (Vermilion, 2015)

Robert M. Sapolsky, **Why Zebras Don't Get Ulcers** (St Martin's Press, rev ed. 2004)

Dr Deepak Chopra, **The Seven Spiritual Laws Of Success: A Practical Guide to the Fulfillment of Your Dreams** (Bantam Press, 1996)

Sharon Begley, **The Plastic Mind** (Constable, 2009)

CHAPTER 4

Jon Kabat-Zinn, **Full Catastrophe Living: How to cope with stress, pain and illness using mindfulness meditation** (Piatkus Books, rev ed. 2013)

Mark Williams & Dr Danny Penman, **Mindfulness: A Practical Guide to Finding Peace in a Frantic World** (Piatkus Books, 2011)

Chade-Meng Tan, JOY ON DEMAND: The Art of Discovering the Happiness Within (Harper Collins, 2017)

CHAPTER 5
Don Richard Riso & Russ Hudson, **Personality Types: Using the Enneagram for Self-Discovery** (Houghton Mifflin, 1996)

Sandra Maitri, **The Spiritual Dimension of the Enneagram: Nine Faces of the Soul** (Jeremy P Tarcher, 2001)

Daria Halprin, **The Expressive Body in Life, Art, and Therapy: Working with Movement, Metaphor and Meaning** by (Jessica Kingsley, 2008)

Beatrice Chestnut PhD, **The 9 Types of Leadership: Mastering the Art of People in the 21st Century Workplace** (Post Hill Press, 2017)

Tony Hsieh, **Delivering Happiness: A Path to Profits, Passion and Purpose** (Business Plus, 2010)

Brene Brown, **The Gifts Of Imperfection** (Hazelden FIRM, 2018)

Eckhart Tolle, **The Power of Now: A Guide to Spiritual Enlightenment** (Mobius, 2001)

Eckhart Tolle **A New Earth: Create a Better Life** (Penguin, 2009)

Robert K. Greenleaf , Larry C. Spears , et al., **The Power of Servant-Leadership** (Berrett-Koehler, 1998)

At BUILD+BECOME we believe in building knowledge that helps you navigate your world.

Our books help you make sense of the changing world around you by taking you from concept to real-life application through 20 accessible lessons designed to make you think. Create your library of knowledge.

BUILD + BECOME

www.buildbecome.com
buildbecome@quarto.com

@buildbecome
@QuartoExplores

Using a unique, visual approach, Gerald Lynch explains the most important tech developments of the modern world – examining their impact on society and how, ultimately, we can use technology to achieve our full potential.

From the driverless transport systems hitting our roads to the nanobots and artificial intelligence pushing human capabilities to their limits, in 20 dip-in lessons this book introduces the most exciting and important technological concepts of our age, helping you to better understand the world around you today, tomorrow and in the decades to come.

Gerald Lynch is a technology and science journalist, and is currently Senior Editor of technology website TechRadar. Previously Editor of websites Gizmodo UK and Tech Digest, he has also written for publications such as *Kotaku* and *Lifehacker*, and is a regular technology pundit for the BBC. Gerald was on the judging panel for the James Dyson Award. He lives with his wife in London.

GERALD LYNCH

BUILD + BECOME

GET TECHNOLOGY

BE IN THE KNOW.
UPGRADE YOUR FUTURE.

KNOW TECHNOLOGY TODAY, TO EQUIP YOURSELF FOR TOMORROW.

Using a unique, visual approach to explore philosophical concepts, Adam Ferner shows how philosophy is one of our best tools for responding to the challenges of the modern world.

From philosophical 'people skills' to ethical and moral questions about our lifestyle choices, philosophy teaches us to ask the right questions, even if it doesn't necessarily hold all the answers. With 20 dip-in lessons from history's great philosophers alongside today's most pioneering thinkers, this book will guide you to think deeply and differently.

Adam Ferner has worked in academic philosophy both in France and the UK, but much prefers working outside the academy in youth centres and other alternative learning spaces. He is the author of *Organisms and Personal Identity* (2016) and has published widely in philosophical and popular journals. He is an associate editor of the Forum's *Essays*, and a member of Changelings, a North London fiction collaboration.

ADAM FERNER

BUILD + BECOME

THINK DIFFERENTLY

OPEN YOUR MIND.
PHILOSOPHY FOR
MODERN LIFE.

PHILOSOPHY IS ABOUT OUR LIVES AND HOW WE LIVE THEM.

Using a unique, visual approach to explore the science of behaviour, *Read People* shows how understanding why people act in certain ways will make you more adept at communicating, more persuasive and a better judge of the motivations of others.

The increasing speed of communication in the modern world makes it more important than ever to understand the subtle behaviours behind everyday interactions. In 20 dip-in lessons, Rita Carter translates the signs that reveal a person's true feelings and intentions and exposes how these signals drive relationships, crowds and even society's behaviour. Learn the influencing tools used by leaders and recognize the fundamental patterns of behaviour that shape how we act and how we communicate.

Rita Carter is an award-winning medical and science writer, lecturer and broadcaster who specializes in the human brain: what it does, how it does it, and why. She is the author of *Mind Mapping* and has hosted a series of science lectures for public audience. Rita lives in the UK.

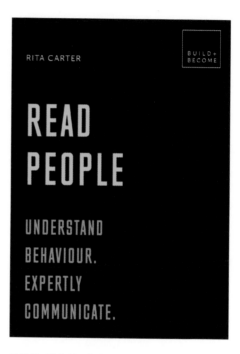

RITA CARTER

BUILD +
BECOME

READ PEOPLE

UNDERSTAND
BEHAVIOUR.
EXPERTLY
COMMUNICATE.

CAN YOU SPOT A LIE?

Using a unique, visual approach, Nathalie Spencer uncovers the science behind how we think about, use and manage money to guide you to a wiser and more enjoyable relationship with your finances.

From examining how cashless transactions affect our spending and decoding the principles of why a bargain draws you in, through to exposing what it really means to be an effective forecaster, *Good Money* reveals how you can be motivated to be better with money and provides you with essential tools to boost your financial wellbeing.

Nathalie Spencer is a behavioural scientist at Commonwealth Bank of Australia. She explores financial decision making and how insights from behavioural science can be used to boost financial wellbeing. Prior to CBA, Nathalie worked in London at ING where she wrote regularly for *eZonomics*, and at the RSA, where she co-authored *Wired for Imprudence: Behavioural Hurdles to Financial Capability*, among other titles.

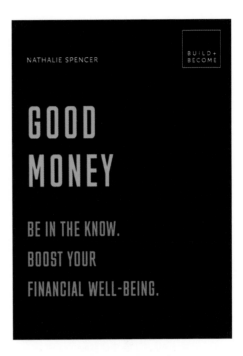

NATHALIE SPENCER

BUILD + BECOME

GOOD MONEY

BE IN THE KNOW.
BOOST YOUR
FINANCIAL WELL-BEING.

WE ALL MAKE CHOICES
WITH MONEY –
UNDERSTAND YOURS.

Through a series of 20 practical and effective exercises, all using a unique visual approach, Michael Atavar challenges you to open your mind, shift your perspective and ignite your creativity. Whatever your passion, craft or aims, this book will expertly guide you from bright idea, through the tricky stages of development, to making your concepts a reality.

We often treat creativity as if it was something separate from us – in fact it is, as this book demonstrates, incredibly simple: creativity is nothing other than the very core of 'you'.

Michael Atavar is an artist and author. He has written four books on creativity – *How to Be an Artist, 12 Rules of Creativity, Everyone Is Creative* and *How to Have Creative Ideas in 24 Steps – Better Magic.* He also designed (with Miles Hanson) a set of creative cards *'210CARDS'*.

He works 1-2-1, runs workshops and gives talks about the impact of creativity on individuals and organizations. www.creativepractice.com

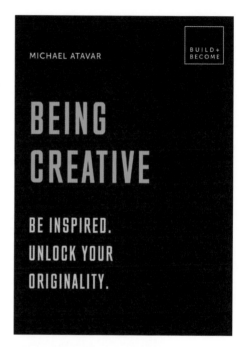

MICHAEL ATAVAR

BUILD + BECOME

BEING CREATIVE

BE INSPIRED. UNLOCK YOUR ORIGINALITY.

CREATIVITY BEGINS WITH YOU.

We are living longer than ever and, thanks to technology, we are able to accomplish so much more. So why do we feel time poor? In 20 eye-opening lessons, Catherine Blyth combines cutting-edge science and psychology to show why time runs away from you, then provides the tools to get it back.

Learn why the clock speeds up just when you wish it would go slow, how your tempo can be manipulated and why we all misuse and miscalculate time. But you can beat the time thieves. Reset your body clock, refurbish your routine, harness momentum and slow down. Not only will time be more enjoyable, but you really will get more done.

Catherine Blyth is a writer, editor and broadcaster. Her books, including *The Art of Conversation* and *On Time*, have been published all over the world. She writes for publications including the *Daily Telegraph*, *Daily Mail* and *Observer* and presented *Why Does Happiness Write White?* for Radio 4. She lives in Oxford.

CATHERINE BLYTH

BUILD +
BECOME

ENJOY
TIME

STOP RUSHING.

BE MORE PRODUCTIVE.

TIME IS NOT MONEY.
TIME IS YOUR LIFE.

Mathematics is an indispensable tool for life. From the systems that underpin our newsfeeds, through to the data analysis that informs our health and financial decisions, to the algorithms that power how we search online – mathematics is at the heart of how our modern world functions.

In 20 dip-in lessons, *Understanding Numbers* explains how and why mathematics fuels your world and arms you with the knowledge to make wiser choices in all areas of your life.

Rachel Thomas and **Marianne Freiberger** are the editors of *Plus* magazine, which publishes articles from the world's top mathematicians and science writers on topics as diverse as art, medicine, cosmology and sport (plus.maths.org).

Rachel and Marianne have co-authored the popular maths books *Numericon* and *Maths Squared*, and were editors on *50: Visions of Mathematics*. Between them they have nearly 30 years of experience writing about mathematics for a general audience.

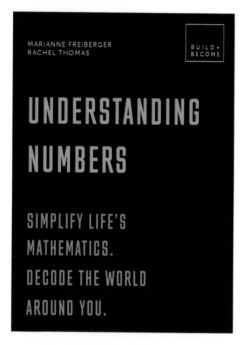

MATHEMATICS IS AT THE HEART OF OUR WORLD.

Disagreements are a fact of life. Productive disagreements are a rarity. We find ourselves living in a divided world in which it's increasingly difficult to have productive arguments.

In 20 thought-provoking discussions, philosophers Adam Ferner and Darren Chetty examine some of today's most pressing debates in politics, society and education. Opening up conversations about conversation, they offer helpful ways to navigate personal and political conflicts.

Adam Ferner has worked in academic philosophy both in France and the UK, but much prefers working outside the academy in youth centres and other alternative learning spaces. He has written two books, *Organisms and Personal Identity* (2016) and *Think Differently* (2018), and has published widely in philosophical and popular journals. He is an associate editor of the Forum's *Essays*, and a member of the Changelings, a North London fiction collaboration.

Darren Chetty has published academic work on philosophy, education, racism, children's literature and hip-hop culture. He is a contributor to the bestselling book, *The Good Immigrant*, co-author of *What Is Masculinity? Why Does It Matter? And Other Big Questions* and co-editor of *Critical Philosophy of Race and Education*.

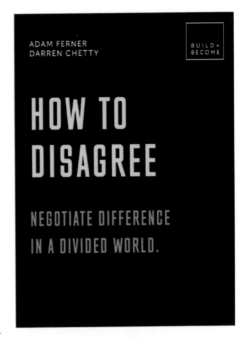

ADAM FERNER
DARREN CHETTY

BUILD +
BECOME

HOW TO DISAGREE

NEGOTIATE DIFFERENCE IN A DIVIDED WORLD.

HOW CAN WE DISAGREE PRODUCTIVELY?

ACKNOWLEDGEMENTS

In writing this book I would like to acknowledge that the lessons contained here have come to me over many years via various wonderful guides, wise traditions, chance conversations, research, client interactions and through my own meditations. In particular, I wish to honour my meditation teacher Georgina Eden, whose power of insight continues to astound and inspire me.

In sharing these lessons here, I do so with huge respect and in deep gratitude for the authors and ancestry of the wisdom contained within.

Special thanks must go to Jessica Axe, who generously invited me to Quarto and believed in my fledgling ideas. To the Commissioning Editor, Lucy Warburton, thank you for offering your eagle eye and brilliant mind – I can confidently say that this book is vastly improved thanks to you. To my Editor, Emma Harverson – thank you for bringing the whole project together with such patience and panache!

And finally, to Jack Newman, Sachi Doctor, Adrian Seligman, David Benjamin Tomlinson and the always patient Ty (our chocolate Labrador) whose feedback, encouragement and loving companionship throughout the process has been just what I needed.

Neil Seligman is a an international mindfulness advocate, conscious visionary and author. He is the Founder of The Conscious Professional, the author of *100 Mindfulness Meditations* and the originator of Soul Portrait Photography. Neil specializes in delivering inspiring keynotes, workshops and seminars on Conscious Leadership, mindfulness and resilience to busy professionals.
www.theconsciousprofessional.com